Broken TOYS

Robert Gatz

Copyright © 2024 Robert Gatz
All rights reserved
First Edition

NEWMAN SPRINGS PUBLISHING
320 Broad Street
Red Bank, NJ 07701

First originally published by Newman Springs Publishing 2024

ISBN 979-8-89308-612-6 (Paperback)
ISBN 979-8-89308-613-3 (Digital)

Copyright: Lyrics © CONEXION MEDIA GROUP, INC.,
HORI PRO ENTERTAINMENT GROUP
Writer: GARY STEFAN HARRISON, GLORIA
JEAN THOMAS, J. D. MARTIN

Printed in the United States of America

To Timber, Adam, Courtney, and Catherine with love.
Thank you for all your support!

Childhood should be carefree, playing in the sun; not living a nightmare in the darkness of the soul.

—Dave Pelzer

Such a pretty little face,
With a heart that's been torn.
Living in a borrowed space,
From the moment she was born.
How many times she's cried,
But never tears of joy.
Someone's taken a little girl, and made a broken toy.

Two sad little eyes,
Painted heartbreak blue.
The simplest of his dreams,
Never will come true.
Someone else's pain,
Fell on this little boy.
Someone's taken a soldier,
And made a broken toy.

Broken toys,
Who will mend these broken toys?
For every one we break,
A broken life takes its place.
That one day will break toys of its own.
O Lord, we've got to mend these broken toys.
And let them be children again,
Give back the innocence stolen from them.
Broken toys,
Who will mend these broken toys?
For every one we break,
A broken life takes its place.
That one day will break toys of its own.
O Lord, we've got to mend these broken toys.

A Fairy-Tale Beginning

Who doesn't love a good story? There's nothing more exciting in our childhood as a really great fairy tale. As we get older, we seek out romance, crime, drama, comedy, or horror, but there is always a part of us that still yearns for the fairy tales we loved as kids. We can become a part of a tale that will take us to lands we'll probably never visit or be involved in the evolution of people and things that are well beyond what we might normally experience.

Once upon a time—that's how fairy tales begin, right? It's a beautiful land that's far, far away from where we live. There's a princess born, a loving father, a mother who has been taken too soon. A wicked stepmother enters, and there are dragons and battles, sorrow and pain, until one day, a handsome prince rides in on a white stallion to save the day. We love the suspense, the action, the drama, but we ultimately look forward to that happy ending, where everything works out for the character we've been rooting for through the pages.

Most horror stories unfold in a similar way. There's an innocent kid living in some small town where life seems perfect—sunshine, happiness, maybe a puppy. Then enters the villain. It's a creepy clown or some kind of menacing creature crawling out of the fog. There's still a battle, and things seem totally lost—very bleak and dark—until the hero, who will save the day, enters. He or she will fight the monster, save the day, and everyone will live happily ever after. The end. I mean that's what most of us want for the character that we invest so many hours in, I assume—a happy ending or at least a temporary conclusion that leads us to the sequel.

I have a story that's neither fairy tale nor horror. There's some romance, a little action, lots of drama, a dash of happiness along the way, crimes, sorrow, and a lot of pain. It's a tale that's full of twists and turns, ups and downs, and though there's a lot of darkness, there's also light. And there's definitely a wicked stepmother. I mean what story doesn't need a good antagonist or two? There's also some monsters, though maybe not the kind with fangs and claws that creep out of the night, and there are plenty of battles throughout. I'll let you decide whether there's a happy ending or not.

I was born on a wintry day in 1966 amidst the turmoil of the Vietnam War. Lyndon B. Johnson was president, and the nation was torn over this war, which would not be entirely over until 1975. My birth name was Robert, but my family called me Bobby. I never understood why they named me one thing and then called me a completely different name, although it was kind of fitting because I would grow up feeling like two different people.

I'm told I was fighting against facing the world as Darlene, my mom, paced the hallway, trying to encourage the birth of her third child. If I had known what the years ahead were going to bring, I would have fought even harder to stay in the safety of her womb. By the time I was conceived, my mother had fallen out of love with Eddie, my dad. She said she would never change having me, but she felt awful for bringing me into an already-troubled home in the middle of a small town in Central Oklahoma. The birth of another child would not fix the marriage any more than the other two children had.

Mom and Dad met in 1957 and had their first date in a local café in Union City right after their senior trip. They dated off and on until April 1959. They had gone to a rattlesnake hunt in Okemah, and the next day, my dad offered her an engagement ring. She knew he drank a lot and was rumored to have several girls at any given time, but she loved him and believed she could change him, so she accepted. They were married in a Catholic church in June. The wedding day was a foreshadowing of the rest of their life together because Dad showed up late and drunk with another girl by his side. Perhaps Mom should have realized she was making a mistake and run for the hills, but if she had, I would not be here to tell our story.

In September, the draft pulled Dad into the army, and he was sent to Fort Riley, Kansas. He was in the army for a little over two years, and they began to work on having a family soon into the marriage. In 1960, Joe, my eldest brother was born. He came into the world while Dad was out drinking with his brother.

A child did not do much to change my dad or settle him down. He still drank most nights until he passed out in his recliner, and it was not unusual for him to stay gone overnight. Mom would sit up until morning, worrying whether he was dead or alive, but he always showed up eventually, smelling of whiskey and with the faint scent of perfume from other women.

Mom did everything she could think of to be a good wife and mother. She learned how to cook some of Dad's favorites from his sisters and would have the table loaded with food every night, although most of the time, his dinner ended up in the oven wrapped in foil because he was late or did not come home. She cooked, kept the house as clean as she could while raising a baby with no help, and when he wanted to be intimate, she never turned him away as she tried to forget the smell of the women she had washed from his clothes. She still clung to the hope that he'd realize how much she loved him and would change, but nothing was ever enough to keep him home or stop his drinking.

She got to the point that she would lock him out of the house when he didn't come home, but after having to replace several doors that he kicked in, she stopped. He would become mean and angry if she asked him where he had been. This anger led to slaps or shoves that followed with flowers or a gift to say he was sorry. He was always sorry and promised it would not happen again, and it didn't…until the next time.

She finally confided in his brother's wife and cried, asking what more she could do to stop the drinking and abuse. She admitted that she wanted to leave him but was shocked by a slap from her sister-in-law. "Darlene"—my aunt sighed—"if you want to have a good marriage, you just have to let him do whatever he wants to do. Be grateful that he comes home to you."

Mom assumed her sister in-law had resigned herself to the same life.

The home they lived in was where his family raised him, and it was in a state of disrepair. Dad promised he would get around to fixing everything but never found the time. It was not unusual to turn the light on and find a rattlesnake coiled on the steps leading upstairs or to open a drawer and find a snake in it. One day, as Mom went to start a bath, she found a snake waiting in the tub. It became a ritual to always turn a light on before entering a room and being cautious before reaching into corners and cabinets. Mom tried to convince herself that their life was normal.

In 1963, she found out she was pregnant with my sister, Darla. Mom said she felt like she was carrying a large watermelon in her belly. She said she got so large, she felt like she waddled like a duck when she walked.

If she believed that this pregnancy would change things, she was wrong. Things only got worse instead of better. Dad stayed gone for several days at a time, and she had no option but to sit at home and pray he would come home. She said her love died on New Year's Eve of 1964. She fixed dinner, dressed up as best an eight-months-pregnant woman could, and waited for him to come home after work. As the night progressed, she finally reached out to his sister, who came over to wait with her. They watched Buddy Hackett and Johnny Carson, but Dad never came home. He didn't return for two days.

Darla was born a month later without her dad because no one could find the bar he was at. If one child didn't help, a second one only meant more work for Mom. Dad stayed away more and more, and when he was home, she was always in a battle with the man she wanted to love. Instead, she became used to the verbal arguments that resulted in screaming and often led to physical fights that left her feeling broken. One fight ended with her nose broken. Another resulted in a broken eardrum. Next was a broken rib. The doctor asked her with concern if everything was okay at home, and she assured him she was just clumsy. Clumsy in the man she had chosen to marry, she thought.

A little over a year after my sister was born, Mom found out she was pregnant again. Feeling like she had no one to talk to, she started telling one of their best friends about how she felt trapped in a loveless marriage. He and his wife went to the bars with her and Dad when she was allowed to go, and they spent a lot of time together.

One night, when they sat alone at the table, Mom confided in him. "I love my kids," Mom began, "and I once loved my husband very much, but I just can't take any more of the abuse!"

Henry held her as she wept uncontrollably. "Darlene," he said quietly, "I'm not one to tell you what to do because I have plenty of problems in my own marriage, but you have to figure this out."

"Pack your kids up," he continued, "and get out."

"I can't," Mom sobbed. "If I ever took the kids away, he'd never stop until he found me. He would kill me. I believe he loves the kids and wouldn't do anything to hurt them, but if I took them away, he'd be furious. He's even said that I could leave whenever I wanted, but if I took the kids, he'd hunt me down and kill me in front of them."

Henry tried to console her. "That is why you have to leave. Love yourself enough to take care of yourself."

"If I stay," she said cautiously, "I think one of us is going to kill the other one."

"Eddie has no idea what he's got in you," Henry continued. "You are beautiful, and no other woman would put up with all his bullshit for as long as you have!"

They would share their hurts and marital problems with one another over the next year. Though there was no magic wand that could fix anything, it felt great for both of them to at least have someone to talk to and, when necessary, a shoulder to cry on.

In late February 1966, on a night filled with snow and howling winds, I was, with a lot of coaxing and a little castor oil, born to a broken home and a loveless marriage. Mom had already resigned herself that nothing was going to change in the marriage, and I became another burden for her to deal with. She loved me but was weary from fighting for survival. She had long forgotten her hope for happiness or a storybook marriage. Now, she just wanted to survive. She tried to focus on her three children, but the evenings after bedtime while she watched the clock were unbearable. She was terrified of what she'd do if he didn't come home but also feared what would happen when he did. She never knew what she might say that would set him off. She found herself trying to cover up the bruises and having to patch the holes he'd put in the walls with his fist.

She and Henry met more and more to talk about their troubled marriages and try to figure out a solution for both of them. Mom said it was not romantic at that point. The thing she wanted least was another man to trust. It was two friends trying to encourage the other through another day. A sort of friendly love grew from that as their friendship deepened. He began writing poems to encourage her and lift her spirits.

One day in early August of 1966, Henry offered a solution. "We leave together," he began. "No matter how bad my wife is, I won't ever get custody of my kids, and since you fear that if you take your children you'll be killed, we'll leave together. We can go wherever and as far as we need to go for safety. I'll leave as soon as you are settled if you want me to."

Mom shook her head. "I don't think I can leave my babies."

"You said that if you stayed, one of you was going to kill the other," Henry pressed. "What will that solve, and how will that affect your kids? You said you can't take the kids because he'll hunt you down and kill you. I don't know if you have that many choices left."

"I'll have to think about it before I decide," she said through tears.

"Take all the time you need," Henry said comfortingly. "I'm here if you need out."

It only took a few weeks. Bruises on her arms, legs, and face reminded her what she was up against. After his last two-nighter being away, she realized that nothing was ever going to change, and no one in his family truly listened or offered help. She tried to convince herself that if she left, he would get his life together for his kids.

The next night after Dad passed out, Mom crept upstairs to lie with each of us. "You may never understand why I'm doing this"—Mom wept quietly—"but I pray you always know how much I love you! I'm doing this with the hope it will ultimately make things better for you!"

She tucked the covers around us, kissed us each on the forehead, and turned to walk into the heat of the night with one suitcase, her purse, and $100 in cash. She was numb, scared, uncertain. She walked down the dirt road to where Henry sat in the car, waiting. They drove into the unknown future in a friend's borrowed car. They left the vehicle parked in a predesignated place and took a taxi to the bus station. The bus took them to Arkansas, then to Kansas, and the journey ended in Oregon. They decided to stay together for now.

Mom cried for weeks after arriving in Oregon. It got so bad that Henry threatened to put her on a bus and send her back home. She finally pulled herself up, brushed herself off, told herself she did what she had to do, and tucked us safely in a corner of her mind so she could try to start her life over again. She prayed we'd be happy and safe. This is what she had to believe would happen, or she'd go insane.

Henry and Darlene grew closer with each day as they leaned on each other for support. She gradually learned to trust again and opened herself up to love. What they had wasn't perfect, but it was without the violence and screaming she'd grown accustomed to. She never forgot she had three children many states away, but she silently prayed their father would stop drinking and find someone who would love them as their own. She reached out to her mother after some time and checked in to see if she had any news on any of us. Eventually, Dad cut off contact with any of them, so they only had limited information from time to time.

Dad dealt with it the only way he could—with anger. He gathered all of her things in the yard and set them on fire, trying to burn away his feelings of loss and abandonment. There was no consoling him, and his drinking only grew worse. His family gathered to try to do what they could to help, and his mom pulled what she could salvage out of the pile of debris for us kids when we got older.

I knew of my mother only what I heard from my father. She was a lying bitch and a whore who was never fit to be a wife or a mother to anyone. I was the reason she finally left because she never wanted me. He hoped she'd gotten what she deserved. She'd taken his money and the fur coat he'd worked so hard to buy her.

That's all I heard over so many years, but something deep inside told me it wasn't true. There was a voice whispering inside, maybe that of my mom's from the night she left, that said no matter why she left, she did what she believed she had to, and it didn't mean that she didn't love us. I had to cling to this no matter how unbelievable it might seem. It was this that would help me survive my long journey through a miserable childhood.

Cinderfella and the Wicked Stepmother

> I'm a child who was abused. I know the difference.
> I clearly know the difference. The whipping for
> correction and then there's child abuse.
>
> —Tyler Perry

When Mom left, my brother and sister were placed in a Catholic orphanage, but I was too young, so I went to live with my aunt Millie and uncle Eldon. They already had three boys who were older, but they still welcomed me into their home. I don't think I really understood why I was there or where my mother had gone, but one day, I'd look back and realize what an oasis it was for me. Those were probably the happiest memories of my childhood.

Uncle Eldon seemed like a giant to me. He was tall and wide with big hands that swallowed my tiny fingers. My best memory was of him sitting in his favorite armchair as I lay with my head resting on his chest. The sweet smell of his pipe was comforting as he held me while reading his daily paper. All felt right in the world as I felt the rise and fall of his chest. He drank his coffee, and I sometimes got a cup, although it was a very diluted one or maybe just hot chocolate, but I felt like I was being treated like a big boy and drinking coffee with my uncle!

Aunt Millie was a gentle spirit. She always had a smile that could light the room, and I loved to hear her laugh. I remember most the wonderful piles of food she'd make. They lived on a farm, so there was fresh milk, eggs pulled from the nest instead of off the shelf, and meat that had been grown right there on the farm. I can remember the smells from the meals she prepared as they lingered in the house. There was always a bucket beside the stove that held scraps for the bird dogs in the pen outside. Their house smelled warm, inviting, and safe. Every time I would see her after that, I would listen to her laugh as she talked about finding me in the refrigerator one morning with a dozen eggs cracked on the floor and a satisfied grin on my face.

I can still remember sleeping on a pallet in the living room in front of a fire with their Boston terrier, Peggy. We were the best of friends, and one of us was always following the other around wherever we went and whatever we did. For me, it was just as good as the most comfortable bed. They had three sons—Sonny, Johnny, and Jimmy—and they all treated me like one of their own. For me, it was as much like home as it would ever be again.

After I did go back to live with Dad, he allowed me to spend summers there for a while, and I can remember lying on the bed in the room just up the stairs from the kitchen with the sound of a train's whistle riding in on the cool breeze through the open window. The air smelled fresh, and I felt safe. I would bring a book or two for my time there so I could explore distant lands filled with mystery and magic. I could become the protagonist and experience what they did, and when I became scared or weary from the struggles, I could simply close the pages and return when I was ready. If only life could have been that easy!

I had a baby blanket that I carried with me everywhere, and when it was time to wash, Aunt Millie could not pry it away from me. She eventually had to convince me to allow her to cut it in half so I could sit on the washer while one part got cleaned, and I could cling to the other.

One morning, I woke up with a cough and tickling in my throat. I was gagging and coughing so much that Aunt Millie took me to the doctor. The doctor checked my throat but saw no signs of infection, and I did not have a temperature, so he recommended she take me home and watch me. On the way to her house, she asked if I thought ice cream would help. Of course, I said yes. We pulled into the local drive-in, and as she ordered, I coughed a few times, gagged a little, and with a final cough, I reached into the back of my mouth and started pulling out a string. It was from my blanket, and apparently, when I was sucking on it the night before, I swallowed a string. Her laughter and sigh of relief filled the car.

One afternoon, my uncle Eldon took me to Red Rooster, a local ice-cream store, to get something cold on a hot summer day. I got my favorite, a pumpkin ice-cream cone, and as we pulled out, my uncle looked at me, grinning. "You better not get any of that on my new seat." He laughed.

We made it back to the house, and not one drop was on his seat, although my chest and legs were covered. He bellowed with laughter as he grinned down at me. I did everything I could to do what I was told. I wanted to be good.

I lived with my aunt and uncle just short of a year. One day, my dad showed up, and as I ran into his arms, he held me close and whispered something that would change my life forever. He was getting remarried, and I'd have a new mommy. I know my life would have been vastly different if I could have grown up with my aunt Millie and uncle Eldon.

It was great at first being back with Dad and my new mother. I remember Marcella, my stepmother, coming home in her white nurse uniform with a snack for each of us. She had a fancy updo of black hair, which I would learn many years later was a wig; her skin was a slightly darker shade of white than her uniform; she smelled of Chantilly perfume; and she had bright red lips. One year, we had our neighbor bake her a pink cake for her birthday, and she seemed genuinely happy.

Paradise did not last very long, though. One day, she came home furious because she had been fired from her job. We never knew the full details of what happened. "Stupid sons a bitches don't know what they lost," she growled.

She became angry and sullen. It was as if she was transforming into someone else. She began drinking more and smoked all the time. This was the birth of an evil creature that would haunt the rest of my childhood. I never really believed in monsters that lived under the bed, but they would be my best friends as I pushed against the wall to hide with them and the dust bunnies that lived beneath my bed. Even they were scared to face the wrath of my stepmother.

Both of our parents chain-smoked and had a continually growing addiction to alcohol. They smoked so much that when they were home, there were constant layers of smoke throughout the house. It was not unusual for them to go through three or four cases of cigarettes in a week. We would occasionally start cleaning the kitchen walls, and what looked like yellow paint became white with the help of 409 and a lot of elbow grease. The only bad thing was once you started, you had to make it to completion.

There was no reprieve in the car either. No cracked windows for fear smoke might escape and we would be able to breathe. I spent a lot of time in the floorboard, pretending I had fallen asleep and slid off the seat just so I could get below the smoke to breathe freely. I am sure we all smelled like we had just smoked a carton of cigarettes, and someone in the family had. Marcella's drink of choice was Coors and later Coors Light, and Dad favored Old Charter whiskey and Coke when he wasn't drinking beer.

I started kindergarten, and most of my memories from that time were fairly good. In first and second grade, as things began to change in our home, I struggled with *N*s on my report card for not paying attention and talking too much. This got me free passes to the principal's office where I got spankings, and once word got to my parents, I had a punishment waiting on me from my stepmother. Rather than changing my behavior, I continued to act out more and more in school.

Punishments began as regular spankings in my bedroom or standing in the corner of the front hallway. There were times she would make me stand in the corner of the entryway with my nose touching the wall until my dad got home or she decided I had spent long enough there. She would periodically come by to check to make sure I was pressed into the corner. Like a predator, she was silent until she was close enough that I could smell her perfume or the alcohol and cigarettes on her breath. She would slap me in the back of the head, slamming my face into the wall if she didn't feel my nose was touching; or if I was wearing shorts, she'd hit me with the flyswatter on the back of my bare legs. It was for hours sometimes, and all I could do was stand as still and quiet as possible and try to will my dad to come home or pray for it to end. Sometimes I would try to imagine I was someone else or in another place under different circumstances, but time seemed to slow down while I was in the corner. I'd stood there so many times crying that I could smell my salty tears on the wall.

There were brief moments of salvation in my childhood, though they did fade as I grew older. One of those moments happened with my dad. I don't know my age or what I had done, but Marcella felt it was his turn to punish me. This was probably when I was young because she seemed to gain pleasure from doling out the punishment herself. He took me into their bedroom and locked the door. He then sat me down and told me that he wanted me to do better, but he wasn't going to spank me. He had his belt lying on the bed. I was not sure what he meant, but he continued to tell me that he was going to hit the bed but that no one could know he didn't follow through with the punishment. I nodded to assure him I understood. He slapped the bed three or four times and then laid it aside. "Don't do this again, and make sure that no one knows I didn't spank you," he reminded me softly.

I had no problem crying as I left the room because the tears were real. I was touched that there was someone in my life, at least at that moment, who did not want to hurt me. This is the one and only time this happened with him. Maybe Marcella suspected something, or he just refused. He did his fair share of screaming and cussing at me, but he never laid a hand on me, and for that, I was very appreciative for even the smallest amount of kindness.

Another came when a friend invited us to a puppet show. The show was in a church, and before we got into the car, our friend's mom handed us a Bible. Mine was an illustrated Children's Living

Bible. She smiled at me and told me to start with John in the New Testament and then read from the beginning of the New Testament through the end and then start in the Old Testament. I loved reading the stories and looking at the bright pictures that filled the pages. I read any book I could get my hands on, so this was wonderful.

I didn't always understand why people did what they did in the Bible, but I knew that a man came from heaven and was beaten worse than I ever was and then hung on a cross to die. But He came back to save the world. I read exactly the way I was instructed, and it later made sense why she had me do it this way. It seemed that the most important story was about Jesus. That's what the whole Bible looked forward to or back on.

I could look at the pictures and read for hours. It didn't fix anything, but it did give me something like hope. It was faint, but it was there. I can't say I didn't pray that the avenging God of the Old Testament would come and teach Marcella a lesson. I wanted Moses to march to our door and demand that she set me free. Those words gave me a little strength to walk into another day. It was dim, but it was a light in a very dark life.

In school, I was learning bad behavior that would cause me trouble through elementary school. One of my friends taught me how to sneak into the cafeteria and steal cinnamon rolls or cookies while the staff wasn't looking. Fortunately, I never got caught, or I can only imagine what would have happened at home. I already struggled with an unknown watchful eye that reported to my stepmom whether I cleaned my tray or not. I was grilled as to why I didn't eat my vegetables and punished with a spanking or the corner.

Through sixth grade, I would have a problem with taking things like pencils or toys from my fellow students. Most of the time, I wasn't caught but occasionally was sent to the principal and took my spanking that led to another at home. I learned to be as sneaky as possible about it. I didn't need or really want what I took, but I think I was yearning for the life they had rather than the one I lived, and by taking their items, it was like robbing them of a part of what I perceived to be their perfect life.

Learning to read was a nightmare. In the evenings, once my stepmother was home from work, I had to sit right next to her and read aloud. If I missed a word or stuttered trying to figure out how to pronounce something, I received a slap or a twist of my ear. With snot running down my face and tears staining my cheeks, I pushed on reaching for success. If I did well, I did not get a reward, but I certainly got my fair share of punishments. I am not sure why I ended up loving to read with those memories burning in the back of my mind, but I think books opened me up to worlds that were not my own, and I met characters that I wanted so badly to become.

Darla, Joe, and I were playing one afternoon in my sister's room. They thought it would be funny to put me in one of my sister's dresses. "We have another sister," they giggled as I paraded around the room.

We were having a good time and thought it was funny until we heard the door open. We turned, and there was Marcella glaring at us. "Are you a little faggot now?" she spit.

I was probably seven by then and did not know what a faggot was, but I assumed it wasn't good. She grabbed me and led me to the patio door. She shoved me outside in the dress. "You want to be a girl, then you can play outside like one. Don't even think of coming in the house until I say you can."

I was mortified that someone would see me. I tried to shrink against the wall as much as I could. If only it had stopped there!

Her drinking got so bad that it was nothing to hear the pop of a Coors can early in the morning before she started her day. It was her coffee. The abuse started with slaps. I'd say the wrong thing and, in a flash, would feel the sting of her hand on my face. It progressed to twisting my ear until it felt like she was going to rip it from my head. There were plenty of spankings with a belt in the early years that left welts on my legs. You could almost see a gleam in her eyes when she did it, as if she enjoyed inflicting the pain. Maybe it was a power thing. I didn't care either way. I just wanted it to stop. I was nervous all the time, never knowing when she would appear behind me dissatisfied with my performance.

Performance was important. We had chores, and they were expected to be done to her satisfaction by the time she got home from work. Dusting; sweeping and mopping the kitchen and bathrooms; washing and drying dishes; washing and drying laundry and putting it away; ironing my dad's country shirts, jeans, and T-shirts he wore to work; vacuuming the rest of the house; cleaning the bathrooms—I tried to do everything perfectly so she'd be happy with me. I was determined to not have a verbal or physical lashing.

I could never be good enough, though. "You're a lazy little bastard!" she screamed. "Look at this glass."

I looked.

"Do you really think it's clean?"

"Yes, it looks clean to me," I mumbled. I felt the heat of her slap.

"Well, it's definitely not fucking clean!" She pointed to a water spot.

I could see her face change and tried to pull back, but she grabbed me by the ear and began twisting as she pulled me close. I could smell the stench of cigarettes and beer on her breath. There was no beauty in this face, just anger, violence, hatred. "I'm sorry," I sniffled.

"Well, you should be sorry! In fact, you are very sorry. You are a sorry little sad shit who can't do anything right. I work all day, and it's not too much that I expect a clean house when I get home!" She ended this declaration with another slap.

I tried to stand tall, but I could not stop the sobs that wracked my body. My ear was burning. My face felt another sting as she slapped me again.

"I want you to pull every one of those glasses down and wash them again. There better not be one spot when you get done. Do you understand me?"

"Yes ma'am," I managed.

She shoved me away like I was a piece of trash that she could not stand to be so close to. I felt like trash. I tried. I failed. I was bad. I reached for the first glass. I could not seem to do anything right. What was wrong with me?

BROKEN TOYS

My sister and I both had chronic bouts of tonsillitis throughout our childhood, and it was finally decided we needed to get them removed. We were both nervous, but the nurses were nice and did everything to help us relax. I have a birthmark on my upper arm, and the nurses were discussing what it looked like. "I think it's a tornado," said one nurse.

"No," another corrected, "it's Daniel Boone's cap!"

One of the male nurses laughed at them both. "It's obvious that it's an elephant."

I was surrounded by the smell of alcohol, and they reassured me everything would be okay as they placed a mask over my face and said I was going to go to sleep for a little while. I did.

My throat ached when I woke up. I thought it was supposed to make my throat stop hurting. I could still taste the medicine that made me sleep. We were allowed a few ice chips.

"When you get home, you can eat all the ice cream and Popsicles you want," the nurse reassured us. "Your throats will be sore for a while, but hopefully, you won't get as many during the year!"

I got sick, and we had to pull over to the side of the road so I could throw up. That certainly did not make my throat feel any better. Once we got home, we went to sleep in our beds.

The next day I went to take a bath. In the mirror, I could see that the male nurse had been right. He had taken a pen and drawn around my birthmark to illustrate a perfect elephant. I smiled at the gift he had drawn. I remember peach Jell-O and Popsicles. I could not eat ice cream because it made me throw up.

Recovery was slow, but I also got a reprieve from the screaming and hitting. The sore throat was worth it if it meant I was free even for a little while. It did not last long, though. "Bobby, get your ass in here right now," Marcella screamed.

My heart was thrashing inside my chest, and my legs shook. What had I done wrong this time? I stood before my tormentor.

"I thought you dusted today?" she screamed.

"I...I did." I muttered.

"Well, if you had fucking dusted, you would have found this." She held up a piece of paper that she had apparently hidden beneath one of the doilies on the end table.

"I...I'm sorry. I promise I'll do better next time."

"I've had it with your stupid shit. Go to your room."

I went to my bedroom and sat on the bed. Tears fell, although nothing had happened yet—anticipation. The knob rattled, and she stormed in, slamming the door behind her. "Get your belt!" she ordered.

"My belt?" I questioned.

She slapped me. "Yes, dumbass. Get your fucking belt and bring it to me."

I did and handed it to her with trembling hands.

"Take your shirt and pants off."

I had no idea what was happening, but I did what she told me to. This was going to be something new.

"Lean over the bed."

The first lick of the belt was across my lower legs. My knees buckled, and I let out a shocked squeal.

"Stand up, or it's going to get worse!"

The next lash came across my buttocks. I pressed my face into the blanket, trying to muffle my screams. More came—my back, my legs. One, two, three—I stopped counting. I prayed for it to stop. I think she stopped only because she wore herself out.

"Get dressed," she panted. "Next time you'd better make sure you do a better job! You can't do anything right, and this is all your fault! Now stop crying and get dressed before I give you something to cry about."

Seriously? As if what happened was not enough to make me cry!

She left, and I lay with my face pressed into my bed, trying to stifle my sobs so she would not hear me and come back into the room. My whole body felt like it was on fire, and I couldn't stop the trembling. She was right. I was bad. It was my fault. I knew there was something wrong with me and felt like I deserved what happened. I made sure when I dusted that I looked for all those pieces of paper.

It did not matter because she'd always find something that was done *half-ass*, and there would be a repeat.

I tried to pray and ask for help, but it did not make me *feel* any better or safer. I felt as if there was a chasm between me and God. I wanted to believe He was there and listening, but I could not hear His voice. I kept making stupid mistakes that resulted in the punishment Marcella dealt out toward me. I begged God to stop her. I pleaded for Him to *fix* me so I would not be so bad anymore, but He was silent.

One day after an especially harsh thrashing, I was in the yard with my dad, and he pointed to my legs and asked what happened. "I did something wrong, and Momma spanked me," I said with my eyes to the ground.

"Did your brother and sister do this to you," Dad asked.

"No, Mom did this to me." I pulled up my shirt and showed him the welts and bruises on my back.

"That is not a spanking! Are you serious? Your mother did this to you?"

"Yes, Daddy, she did."

"Well, I'll promise you this: she'll never do that to you again!" He turned and stormed into the house.

I felt like I was flying. After so many times, it was finally over! My dad was going to protect me and put a stop to the abuse. But it was not. The next time, she leaned in close and warned me that if I told again, she would make sure I could not stand for a week. She learned to keep the welts and bruises off my lower legs so they would not show in my shorts. I learned to keep my mouth shut.

One spring day, as she washed my sister's hair in the sink with the windows opened, I played with my spirograph downstairs in the den. I could hear the birds singing, and a breeze would occasionally blow through. It was a perfect day…until it was not. I leaned forward to grab a pen and knocked the box in the floor. All the pieces clattered to the ground, and before I could react, she was standing before me. I saw rage and hatred. She grabbed me by the ear and began twisting. "What the fuck?" she screamed. "Is this how you show appreciation for your stuff? We work hard to give you these things!"

"It was an accident," I tried to explain.

Her slap stopped me. She grabbed me by the ear and started twisting so hard, I felt like my ear would come off in her hand. Before I realized what was happening, she was slamming me face-first into the wall. I had never experienced anything like this before. *Let it stop! Let it stop!* I prayed silently.

The fourth or fifth time, there was a pop, and I felt something warm running down my face.

"Oh my god! Look what you've done?" she screamed as if it were my fault. "Lay down on the couch." She grabbed a washcloth and came back to press it to my nose.

For a moment, I thought I felt actual tenderness, but just as I let my guard down, she leaned close to my ear. "If you tell your brother or father about this, I *swear* I will come into your room at night and smother you to death."

All I could do was shake my head in fear. I believed her. It didn't take much imagining to see her standing over me with venom dripping as she wrapped her talons around my throat.

I began wetting my bed at night after this. I was ashamed at first and tried to hide it, but one morning, she caught me putting my sheets and pajamas in the washer. I should have waited until she left.

"It's not time to wash the sheets. What are you doing?" she questioned.

"I…I just wanted to wash them," I stuttered.

"Let me see these." She ripped them out of my hands. She could feel the moisture and smell the urine.

I trembled waiting for her response.

"Did you piss your bed?" she screamed incredulously. "Are you that fucking lazy that you can't get out of bed and go to the bathroom?"

"I had a bad dream. I'm sorry."

"You're a little pissant!" she screamed as I withered before her.

She came in to check my bed every morning after that. Many nights I stayed dry, but the days I did not, she grabbed my ear, twisting, and would rub my face into the wet sheets, as if I were a bad puppy that had piddled in the floor. "Do you like that smell? You must because it isn't that hard to get your ass out of bed and go to the bathroom."

I just stared at the floor with tears running down my face. I was ashamed that I wet the bed, but I could not express the terror that haunted my dreams or the fear of going into the hallway right by her bedroom door with the fear that she would be there waiting for me. As punishment, there were times that she even made me wear the wet underwear so I could remember throughout the day what I had done. I could smell my sin throughout the day.

Sometimes I peed while having a nightmare, but other times, I would wake up and just be too scared to leave the bedroom. On a few of those nights, I'd pee under the bed or in the closet just so I didn't have to go out into the dark hall where I was afraid that she waited to attack me. I prayed I would not get caught because I knew what lived in the darkness outside my room. I was ashamed of what I did, but fear can make us do some crazy things.

For a while, she started coming into my room in the middle of the night and would force me to stand up. She would pull me into the bathroom and have me pull my pajama bottoms and underwear down. Then she would grab my penis and tell me to pee. If I did not produce in the right amount of time, her other hand would swat me on my naked butt, and that only made it harder for me to try to go to the bathroom. Even if I had to pee urgently, I was so ashamed and shocked and scared all at the same time that I couldn't relax enough to make myself go. It made me very uncomfortable for a woman to be holding my penis and commanding me to pee on demand. What would seem like hours would pass, and I finally could squeeze enough out that she would let me go.

It wasn't uncommon to have several rounds of the swats and her threatening me. I felt violated with her hand on my private parts. I wanted to run and hide from her. I wanted someone to save me and stop what was happening. No one ever did.

One morning, when she came in to find that I had wet the bed, she did the usual face rubbing in the sheets and then made me change my underwear and pajamas. She pulled the wet underwear over my head and yanked me to the patio door. She opened the door and shoved me outside. "Let everyone see what a pissant you are! Stay right there until I come back, or you'll be sorry!"

I tried to curl into the smallest ball, pressed against the wall so hopefully no one would see me. My body was wracked with sobs as I silently prayed that she'd reconsider and let me come back inside. I breathed in the smell of what I had done.

After several hours, she finally opened the door and let me back in. I could see the horrified faces of my brother and sister. "Go to your room!"

And if the physical beatings weren't enough, she loved to use words against me to help destroy any remaining self-esteem I might have left. *Pissant* was one of them when I started wetting the bed, but she certainly didn't stop there. I gained some weight for a few years, and so she began calling me "fat ass" or "lard butt." Even as I lost weight, she still used the terms to break me down. She also used pretty much every cuss word that existed to embellish anything she used to describe me. It left a lasting imprint on me because even when I was eighteen and 145 pounds, all I saw when I looked in the mirror was a fat man. My self-image was destroyed.

We had a ritual when we were young on the nights that Dad and Marcella were both home. We'd say good night, tell them we loved them, and give them a kiss. One night as I leaned in to kiss Marcella, she gripped the back of my head and tried to stick her tongue in my mouth. I was too young to realize it was called a French kiss, but I was disgusted at what she'd done. She let me go and then just did her cackling laugh. My dad said something to her. I don't even remember the words because I was in total shock. I was crying when I told him good night.

I was reluctant to go to her after that, but she never tried to do it again. It was like the kiss of Judas when he sealed Jesus's fate. I didn't want to give her a kiss. It meant nothing on most nights because I'd been through some trauma with her, and I never believed there was love behind the kiss or her words. It was a kiss of betrayal.

Marcella was not a terrible cook, but she could make some strange concoctions like creamed onions or pureed liver for sandwiches. She always made our plates, and we had to sit at the table until we finished eating. It felt as if she knew what we liked and gave us very little, but we got plenty of what she knew we wouldn't enjoy. This day, it was green beans with bacon that had been cooked in vinegar. My brother and sister were smart enough that they would blend enough of the bad stuff in, so they didn't end with a plate of something they didn't like, or they had a stronger stomach than I did. I tasted the beans, and the bitterness made me gag. I ate the other things on my plate as I tried to squeeze in a bite of the green beans but just could not swallow it without gagging. My dad, brother, and sister all finished their plates, and I was the only one sitting there, staring at the horrid creation left on my plate.

"You are going to finish every last bite, or you will not leave this table," my stepmother said, and I knew she meant it.

I could just stare at her trying to plead with my eyes to set me free, but she stared back with cold black eyes that held no mercy. I heard my dad listening to *Hee Haw* on the television and tried to focus on that. The longer I sat there, I could see grease congealing on the green beans.

"Eat your fucking beans!" she screamed.

I picked up two beans with my fork and put them in my mouth. The bile rose in my stomach as soon as they touched my tongue. I'm sure my face turned as green as the beans.

"Chew them up and start again!"

I tried chewing them, but with every bite, I gagged a little more. Before I could stop it, I felt the bile fill my mouth.

"You better not spit that out!" she screamed as she got in my face.

Tears quietly slipped down my face, and I tried to swallow, but then it was over. As I tried swallowing, I vomited it out onto my plate. I was terrified. She slapped me so hard, I fell out of my chair, and then she was punching me. Spittle flew from her mouth as she screamed, but I don't even know what she was saying anymore.

Finally, she pulled me back into my chair. "Now eat!" she shouted.

I looked at her with horror. She could not be serious. She would not make me eat my vomit.

"Bobby, I've had enough of your bullshit! Eat your dinner and clean your plate."

"I...I...I can't," I sobbed.

"Damn it, Marcella, leave the boy alone and let him up from the table!" my dad shouted from the living room.

I saw what looked like pure evil fill her face, and she leaned in close. "You are a piece of shit. I should shovel this crap into your mouth, but I'll let you up for now. Your daddy might have saved you this time, but I'll get you! Clean this mess up and get ready for bed. I'll deal with you later."

If that hadn't destroyed my spirit, the next thing did. I'm not sure exactly how old I was, but I was too old for someone to be bathing me. I was nervous and shaking as she eyed my naked body. I was squirming under her hands and accidentally farted. This enraged her, and I cowered beneath her gaze. "You did that on purpose, you little shit," she spit as she administered the first slap on my back. "You did that intentionally just to spite me!"

"I didn't!" I gasped as the air rushed out of me in shock.

"You most certainly did!" she screamed as spittle flew from her mouth, and she raised her hand to strike me across the face.

I tried to duck away from her, but there was no escaping her rage. Her hands hit my naked body wherever they could find a spot. I was terrified, but the worst had not happened. I shit in fear, and then she completely lost it.

"You nasty little bastard! I'm going to teach you a lesson you'll never forget."

Blow after blow struck me, and I don't think there was a single spot on my body she didn't connect with. I was sobbing uncontrollably and could only pray silently for someone to help me. It felt like the hits went on forever, but she finally stopped, gasping for air.

"Clean this mess up and go to bed!"

As I washed the tub and myself, gagging as I watched my feces swirl down the drain. I also watched my hope for a normal childhood go with it. Nothing was normal in my life, and it never would be.

After the beatings, I would lie on my side, shivering and looking at the picture that hung over my bed. It was of an angel standing beside a bridge with a boy and girl on it. They had just passed over a missing board on the bridge. I imagined the girl was my sister, and the little boy was me. The angel was giving them safe passage. Did that angel watch over me? Why did God let these things happen? Did He even know I existed?

"Please, God," I would pray. "Please help me. I can't do this anymore. I don't know why I'm so bad, but I believe You can help me if You want to. Please stop this! Please stop her!"

Maybe He heard my prayers, but there seemed to be no end in sight, and the beatings never stopped. There was not going to be some miracle to save me from my fate. This was my life, and I figured I had done something to deserve it. Even God did not find me worthy of His time or help.

I was still a young child when I died the first time. It was not a physical death but more of a death in my spirit. It was when hope for freedom died, and I knew my life was destined to be this way. No one was going to rescue me, and the abuse was never going to end. I might as well accept my fate. I prayed, but God was silent. He did not feel I was worth saving either.

It got so bad at times that I would sit in the dark utility room hallway with a knife to my chest. I'd plead for the strength to plunge it into my chest. I just wanted the pain to stop.

The only thing that saved me was the little I knew of the Catholic religion. We had crucifixes and the angel picture in my room, but we never went to church. The only time I heard *god* was when it was followed by *damn*. I read somewhere that in the Catholic religion, suicide was considered an unforgiveable sin. I lived in hell every day of my life, but eternity in a real hell did not seem too appealing, so I always resisted the desire to end my life. I felt like a failure. I could not even do this right. At the time, I felt as if maybe it would have just been better to slide the knife in and find some kind of end with even the smallest chance for a little peace. Maybe hell would not have been as bad as what I lived with. Maybe it was God Himself who gave me the strength to hang on, but whatever it was, I held on to what little hope I could muster.

The abuse was not just at home. The verbal and emotional abuse carried with us wherever we went with our parents. At reunions, most of the time, we sat off to the side because we were afraid we'd do something wrong to upset Marcella and then face humiliation at her screaming at us. We had one aunt we confided some of what went on at home when she'd come sit with us, but there was never any intervention. I feel certain that unless everyone was blind, our neighbors and family were aware that something was not right at home, but it was a time when people just didn't interfere in others business, not even if it meant saving a life.

I had one moment in midhigh when I joined a divorce support group. When it came to me, I told, without going into great detail, some of what it was like at home with my stepmother and how I wished my mom was there to take me away from it all. Apparently, that wasn't what they were hoping for in the group because it was canceled the next week—another reminder to keep silent.

I can remember other gatherings we went to with her family, and we were told to not misbehave and to sit still and be quiet. I was told so many times to sit down and shut up, and even when I was not told specifically not to interact with others, I was simply terrified to. Not realizing the reason at the time, this would carry with me even into adulthood where I am uncomfortable in large settings and very awkward most of the time just trying to be friendly and chat with others. I end up sitting off to the side unless someone approaches me and draws me in. There is still a terrified boy inside who just wants to be left alone.

We did enjoy going to two of her sisters' houses and playing with their kids when we were young, but they had a falling out, and we stopped going to visit. We'd also go to her mother and father's house for holidays, and I can remember her mother being so nice to us. She'd send us home with candy or cookies that Marcella ended up taking to work rather than allowing us to have them. It was the same on Halloween. We learned to hide some of the candy because she would take it away and bring it to her coworkers.

I can remember once going out to eat, and the waitress complimented us on our behavior. This set Marcella off, and she started cussing and saying how useless we were at home. I was embarrassed, but I also felt sorry for the poor waitress who was just trying to be nice. Fortunately, we didn't eat out all that much, so we were saved from further shame.

I did not understand why my brother and sister never seemed to get the same treatment. I suspect it was because I was the youngest and most vulnerable. She certainly was no less harsh verbally on them, and there was an occasional physical assault, but it felt like I was alone in the brunt of her anger. My dad was verbally abusive, and he did not protect me, but he never hit me. He saved that for Marcella. Because he didn't stop her, I felt he was giving her permission to continue to administer the abuse.

They fought often and furiously. Our cleaning duties included picking up the broken glasses and ashtrays that had been thrown. There was a lot of screaming and cussing and many times "your fucking kids" was thrown at Dad from Marcella. I often wondered if that's why she was so violent with me. Maybe she was striking out at Dad through me. She couldn't hit him, so she hit me instead. Their fights became physical at times. We fought our instincts, which were to let Dad hit her, but we were always in the battle, trying to pull him off her.

There were times when I paused. The bruises were still fresh, and the welts still stung, but self-preservation was won over by a moral value that said you defend the weaker one. I won't say that I didn't see the irony and the harsh reality that there was no one to protect me. Supernaturally, I might have an angel watching out for me, but physically, no one could stop her.

But Marcella needed someone to protect her from my dad's wrath. "You fucking bitch," my dad screamed as he threw his glass at the wall beside her.

She spat back. "You son of a bitch! That nearly hit my head."

"I wish it would have!" he screamed back.

"You piece of shit!" she yelled. "I should have never married you. You and your fucking kids are nothing but a weight around my shoulders."

"You're a whore, and I should have known better. Everyone knew it," he threw back. "Leave my kids out of this!"

"Your kids are lazy bastards who don't do anything right. They are nothing but useless pieces of shit! I work all day and come home and have to do all the crap they should have taken care of."

"You shut the fuck up!" He rose and stumbled to the kitchen to pour another glass of Old Charter whiskey and Coke.

As he came back in the room, she screamed at him, "You are—"

She didn't finish because he stopped and slapped her.

"You motherfucker!" she screamed as she leapt up to shove him away. "You hit me again, and I'll call the police!"

He shoved her back down. "Sit down and shut up before I rip your face off!"

That was a typical fight, except they went on for hours. We would get up and try to intercede on her behalf when it became too violent. Other times, I would lie in bed with my pillow over my head, praying they'd both shut up. Sometimes I'd rock and kick the wall to try to remind them they had children listening, but nothing stopped their tirades. There were school nights that we were awake until after 2:00 a.m., listening to them fight over anything and everything. Many nights, it was about the *useless kids*. What a way to build self-esteem and promote learning! I have no idea why I had trouble focusing on my schoolwork at times.

She'd leave him notes on nights when he worked late, listing all the ways we failed to live up to her standards and how we'd screwed up again. She challenged him to fix us or threaten to leave him. If only we could have been so lucky.

Each year, I fought to just move forward. I felt like I was in quicksand, and the harder I struggled, the more I sank into the mud.

Nightmares were frequent and intense. I eventually won the battle of wetting the bed, but the damage had been done. In my dreams, I would find myself in a dark room. I knew where the light switches were, but they would not work, so I had to wade through the blackness to find escape. I knew there was something in the inky dark that was coming for me even though I did not see what it was. I fought my way forward with heart pounding and praying I would escape. Many times, I would make it to the exit, but *she'd* be there looming over me. I'd try hitting and shoving my way past her, but she was like a Bozo Bop Bag, and as I punched her, my fist would have no effect as she kept bouncing back up, and her evil laughter would fill the night. Then I would wake up terrified and sweating, trying to remind myself that it was just a bad dream.

Sadly, even my waking hours felt like a nightmare at times but one I could not wake up from. I was void of any self-confidence or feeling of worth. She had stripped me emotionally with each beating and verbal lashing until I was raw, broken, and hated myself. I never really knew why I was the one she turned her anger on, so I believed that I must have done something to deserve all that she did to me. Only as an adult and with a lot of counseling would I realize that no one ever deserves to be treated the way I was. I may have done bad things from time to time, but that did not make me a bad person.

As I turned thirteen, the beatings subsided some and were replaced mostly with just slaps and verbal onslaughts, but I preferred them over the belt. My escape was through the worlds I found in books. I was always reading a book. I had a dresser drawer full of books, and I loved going to the library with the smell of old books. I would sit in the floor, thumbing through the many options, looking for my next adventure. If only for a moment, I was able to escape the reality of *my world* for worlds unknown. I could be a prince searching for a princess, a knight fighting a dragon, a sorcerer who could do real magic, or travel to almost anywhere I would want to go.

It was fifth grade when I became passionate about books. My teacher read us Wilson Rawls's *Where the Red Fern Grows*, and I sat in awe on the floor, listening to the words and seeing the characters come to life in my mind. It opened a new world for me and became my favorite book. After that, I read any book I could get my hands on. I devoured anything by Dean Koontz or John Saul, and I have all of their books to this day. I haven't read all of Stephen King's books but have read many and add at least one every several years. Reading was my escape from a reality I didn't like.

I'd often read with a flashlight under the covers at night when I couldn't sleep. I was reading the book *Jaws* when I was about ten years old. I'd made it a few chapters in when my stepmother found it in my bed. She marched to the library stating a child that young shouldn't be allowed to read something so violent and graphic. The irony was lost on her.

My other escape was television. I'd hurry home from school so we could watch *The Brady Bunch*, *The Partridge Family*, or *Gilligan's Island*. I knew it was unrealistic, but I could be a Brady or Partridge for thirty minutes a day and, for a moment, be in a family where I could feel loved and safe.

I also loved horror movies. Any horror movie I could watch I enjoyed because the monster almost always was defeated. There was nothing more frightening than what I lived with on a daily basis. In 1979, I watched the series *Salem's Lot* while I was home alone. I had the lights off, and though the bathroom was just down the hall, I could not move for the entire show. It was a miniseries, so I had to sit through the terror twice, but it was worth it. Good won over evil. It also had James Kerwin from *James at 15* and David Soul from *Starsky & Hutch*, which were both favorites of mine. If I only had to deal with vampires, it would have been much easier because I couldn't just use a stake to kill my monster, and crosses or holy water had no effect.

One afternoon, I watched a rerun of *Hello, Dolly!* with Barbra Streisand and fell in love. I thought she was not only beautiful but had a voice like an angel. I watched as many of her movies and bought as many of her cassettes as I could. She filled me with joy, and through the music she sang or the stories she told, I would have temporary peace around me. Her voice lifted me from the despair that surrounded me.

I would also walk to the movie theater and watch movies. It was these moments that I could hide from my world and suspend the reality of my life for a few hours. They were breaths of fresh air, even if they did not last.

In 1980, I walked to the theater to watch *9 to 5* with Dolly Parton, Lily Tomlin, and Jane Fonda. I laughed so hard that I went back several more times, and each time, it became funnier than the last. The next year, Lily Tomlin was in *The Incredible Shrinking*

Woman, and the year after that, I watched my first 3D movie starring the unknown Demi Moore in *Parasite*.

Movies and books were the only way I could find to leave my life for a moment. Without them, I would have been more lost than I was.

My freedom finally came in May of 1982. One morning, Dad was still drunk from the night before, and he got in a fight with my sister. I will never forget the fear I felt. He was screaming at her and shoving her against the wall in the bathroom. I had never seen him be physically violent with my sister or me. She was crying, and I was pulling at his arm to get him away from her. Finally, in one last burst of anger, he screamed at her to pack her bags and get out of his house. Shocked, I told him he couldn't do that, and he said that if I didn't like it, I could pack my bags too. He stormed out of the house, and we immediately called our brother, who was able to move out of the house when he was seventeen. He had gotten his own place and married since.

"Good," he said. "Enough of this crap. Pack all you can, and when I get off, I'll come get you. We'll figure something out."

So we did just that. My sister packed and then went to work, and I was alone packing when Dad came back home. He opened my bedroom door and asked what I was doing.

"Packing," I told him. "You told us to get out, so Joe is picking us up, and we are getting out." My heart was racing. Dad had sobered up some, but I did not know what he'd do or how he'd react.

"You'll be sorry for this little stunt you are pulling," he threatened. "This is bullshit!" Dad slammed my bedroom door and got on the phone and then left the house again.

I stayed in my room, nervous and scared, until Joe showed up. We got our things and left. It felt unreal. I could not believe it could be over this easily.

As if it were planned exactly this way, my brother had reunited with our mother in 1981, and I met her for the first time on my sixteenth birthday in February 1982. We still had a few weeks of school left, so we stayed with Joe and his wife, Vanessa. Mom would drive us to school in her brown Volare station wagon and pick us up at the end of the day. I was paranoid at first, thinking I would walk out one day to find Dad and Marcella waiting for me. I was always looking over my shoulder.

Dad and Marcella called all the time, making threats, and they drove by my brother's house, but nothing ever came of it. School was out, and my sister had her graduation. We moved to Texas with our mother, and finally, there was light in my life. I had scars, but they faded a little more each year. I would be forever changed by what happened, but I survived that chapter of my story.

Wolves in Sheep's Clothing

> When someone was hitting me, or like sexually molesting me, it just seemed normal to continue to do that to myself.
>
> —Tatum O'Neal

There is no betrayal quite so hard as that from someone you trust. I knew where I stood at home, so there were very few surprises. If it was hard to fight for survival at home, it was just as bad when I went to school because that is where I should have been able to be protected and safe, but bullies abounded.

I had something that I would not learn about until I got much older. It was gynecomastia, which meant I had prominent breasts for a boy. When I was skinny, I had them, When I was fat, they were bigger. They were always there. This was the perfect thing for a bully, and they loved to torment me with their taunts. "Look," one would tease, "Bobby has breasts just like a girl!"

"Bobby's titties are bigger than my girlfriend's!" shouted another.

"Do you have your training bra?"

And everyone would laugh while I wished I could disappear.

I hated gym class because I was ashamed to be undressed in front of anyone. The pointing and laughing followed me all through school. It was never anything I could just outgrow. I was not athletic enough to fit in with the jocks, too uncool to fit in with the popular crowd, and too quiet for the smart kids, so I kind of fell into the outcasts. I was not entirely alone, but it was a lonely place to be through my school years. I had a few friends but could never truly open myself up to them for fear they would think I was a freak because of the things that happened in my home.

My sophomore through senior years, I embraced journalism and writing and was able to spread my wings a bit but never flew very far beyond where I'd been for most of my school years. Once you become an outcast, you do not really have the luxury of establishing yourself as anything else. It is decided for you by your classmates, and you have no say.

In first grade, I had a couple of classmates who enjoyed picking on me. I could never escape them and their bullying. One day, while we were on recess, I had enough and threw a buffalo I had gotten on a family trip at one of them. Of course, I got in trouble, and once I got home, Marcella gave me a spanking. She and my dad told me that I better never get in a fight at school, or I'd be in trouble once I came home. That stripped me of my defense, so I had to accept the torment as I faced my bullies. And Marcella took my toy buffalo away from me, and I never saw it again.

In second grade, there were several of us playing chase, and as I rounded a corner, a gate that was leaning against the fence fell and hit me in the head. I was dazed, and it hurt, but I did not think it was anything terrible until a girl started screaming that I was bleeding. I put my hand on my head and pulled away, seeing blood. This got me to screaming and drew the attention of a teacher. I was taken to the nurse.

Later in fifth grade, we were playing train or something on the large slide on the playground. As I neared the top and was sitting down, someone shoved me, and I fell over the top onto the ground below. I blacked out for just a second but wasn't seriously hurt.

In twelfth grade, on our senior trip, we went to Six Flags over Texas. As we returned to the bus, I saw kids climbing in the back of the bus through the emergency exit door. I wanted to be cool too, so I tried entering the same way. As I pushed myself up, someone grabbed my wrist and pulled, trying to help me, but it was a little too much, and I hit the top of the door. I fell backward out of the back of the bus and hit my head on the ground. I was not allowed to sleep on the trip home because of fear of concussion. It felt like even the universe hated me at times! I wondered if all the hits to the head had any effect on my future life. At graduation, when my name was called, I stood and heard some of my classmates chanting, "Bang your head." It was probably not meant in kindness, but I did find humor in it and smiled to myself.

In seventh grade, I had a classmate who had tormented me for years. He lived just a few blocks from me, so we rode the same bus, and he would constantly punch the back of my seat. No matter where I sat, he would sit behind me just so he could torment me. I stared forward and ignored him as much as I could. I knew I could not fight back, or I would get in trouble at home.

One afternoon, he followed me off the bus, taunting me. He started poking my backpack as we walked, calling me names. I tried to tune him out, but he shoved, and I fell face forward into the grass. He was about twice my size, but this didn't stop him from climbing on my back. He started punching me and slammed my face into the ground. "Punk," he teased. "You're a little faggot, aren't you?"

I heard a car stop nearby and a woman screaming at him to stop. I felt her pushing him, and he toppled sideways. She leaned over me and asked if I was okay. I did my best to hold back tears. "Yes." I stood up and angrily hit him with my backpack. I did not care if I got in trouble at that point. It got a little better after that, but anytime I saw him, my guard went up, and I tried to steer clear of him.

The neighborhood kids made fun of the shape of my head by calling me *Eggbert*, and since they'd heard how I peed the bed, they teased me about this. I had no escape or safe place to hide. It was torment wherever I turned. The only release I found was in riding my bike or playing in the treehouse that was in our backyard. I would pedal my bike through the summer evenings, listening to the locusts in the trees, feeling the warm breeze around me. I could pretend to be anyone else and forget what was happening around me. Those moments were priceless.

In 1976, the movie *Carrie* came out. It was another terrifying movie from Stephen King. I had read the book as well, which was equally frightening. I sided with Carrie White. She was tormented year after year because she was different and finally sought revenge. Most kids who are troubled in school because of the taunts of classmates do not have telekinetic powers to fight back. Oppression of any people always ends with revolt at some level. People can only take so much.

I hate hearing about the horror of school shootings, and my heart breaks for the innocent lives lost and the parents who are left grieving for their children, but a small part of me can relate to the pain the shooters feel, and I cannot help but wonder what happened to them that they felt like that was their only way out. It was only grace and the absence of a gun that I did not try to get out of my life in a similar way.

Sometimes you are left with what seems like the only choice of taking your own life or striking out at the world around you. It is not right. It is a terrible thing that should never happen to anyone. But it is also something that could possibly be prevented if someone cared enough to intercede. It is easier to ignore what's building until it's too late. Someone who showed enough compassion by stopping the abuse or the bullying could prevent a tragedy that is rooted in some form of mental illness.

An act of kindness early on could change one person's life, and that could lead to changing the lives of many others. It might be as simple as letting someone know they are not alone and are not forgotten. A teacher, a neighbor, a family member—that's all it takes, one person to remind a broken toy that it can be mended. It can be fixed.

I was blessed to have some good teachers along the way who gave me encouragement and showed me kindness, and the few classmates who called themselves my friend gave me the strength to return each day. Two teachers stood out in midhigh school. Both were English teachers, and through their kindness, I learned to embrace writing, and that eventually evolved into my joining journalism and writing for the school newspaper. It was much-needed escape and enjoyment that followed me into high school.

I was quiet and withdrawn and tried to hide in books, which was like putting a target on my back. I was called a nerd, gay, faggot, queer, weirdo, and many other names equally degrading. When the harassment began, I had no idea what most of the names even meant, but I knew it was not meant as a compliment. I was shoved, belittled, and made fun of. It was not enough what happened at home, I had to fight for peace at school as well.

I further withdrew and tried to hide from the other kids so I would not have to deal with the verbal or physical abuse. It made me angry for a while, and I acted out a bit at school, but after dealing with the "spankings" at home after I got in trouble at school, by fourth grade, I had learned to just sit down and shut up. I don't really understand what goes through a person's mind that makes them pick on a defenseless kid who did nothing more than to show up. A child gets picked on because they look different, dress differently, sound different, love differently, or simply because they are quiet. The person who becomes the bully does not ever stop to think about what that child is dealing with at home. Maybe that kid is just trying to survive verbal, physical, emotional, or sexual abuse at home too, and bullying is their way of dealing with it. Would it even matter if the bully knew? Would they think twice before calling you names or pushing you around? I don't know the answer to those questions.

Unfortunately, there are more wolves roaming around in sheep's clothing than just my parents and classmates. Marcella had a nephew named Johnny who would go dancing and drinking with her and Dad on weekends. I think he was in his thirties. Most holidays, he was present, and he was always friendly, making an effort to come and talk with my brother, sister, and me. Oftentimes, he came by after Dad and Marcella had left for the club or bar, and he'd sit and watch television with us for a while or talk. Many times, this would end in horseplay between him and my brother, and they'd sometimes go in the bedroom. I never thought anything of it because he was an adult and someone we knew.

I was twelve the year my brother moved out, and Johnny continued to stop by some weekends when I was alone. It never felt weird to let him in because he was someone I knew who was always coming over. He was an adult I trusted. Sometimes he would talk for a little while and then leave, and other times, he might sit and watch TV with me. Sometimes he would interact with me, tickling playfully or gently wrestling with me on the couch.

One night, this changed. "Is your mom and dad already gone?" he asked.

"Yeah, they left about an hour ago," I told him.

"Is your sister home tonight?" He closed the front door.

"No," I shared, "she's out with some of her friends tonight."

"So what are you doing tonight?" he asked as he sat on the couch next to me.

"Nothing much. I'll probably watch *Love Boat* and *Fantasy Island* in a little bit, but that's about all."

He scooted a little closer and squeezed my leg and then leaned over, pulling me close and tickling me, making me giggle and push back at him. "Maybe I'll stay and watch some TV with you tonight," he told me. "Would you be okay with that?"

"Sure, I don't mind at all. I think that would be fun."

His hand was on my shoulder rubbing. It felt good. "Why don't you lie down, and I'll rub your back for you," Johnny offered.

"Okay."

He rubbed in circles on my back, squeezed a little at the shoulders, and occasionally would tease me with a tickle. I lay across his lap, enjoying the back rub and attention. "Let's take your shirt off so I can really get your back good."

This sounded a little weird, but I had no reason not to do what he asked. I sat up and took my shirt off and then lay back down. He started the same process as before. This went on for a little bit as I watched TV, and we talked a little. He stopped, and I sat back up.

"Bobby, how was that?"

"Good," I nodded. "Thanks."

"Sure, everyone needs a good back rub every once in a while." He rested his hand on my upper leg and squeezed gently. Then he was rubbing my leg. He pulled my leg up and slipped my shoes off as he started rubbing my foot. He would rub a little and then tickle a little. I giggled.

"Do you have a girlfriend yet?" Johnny asked.

"No," I laughed. "I'm not old enough for a girlfriend, and no girls really like me."

"Well, I figured a good-looking kid like you would have two or three."

"Nope, no girlfriend," I answered.

"I can't believe that."

"I'm kinda quiet at school, and kids call me weird."

His hand moved back up to my upper leg, and he started rubbing again. He touched my private area and squeezed gently. I froze, and my heart started pounding.

"Do you play with yourself very often?" Johnny asked.

"What do you mean *play with myself?* Like I ride my bike and play with my toys by myself sometimes."

He laughed. "No. I mean do you ever touch yourself down here." He put his hand back on my privates.

"No." I wasn't sure what he meant and trembled slightly. I was just entering puberty, I think, and had no idea about masturbation.

"You know I love you and would never do anything to hurt you, don't you?"

"Yeah. I don't think you'd try to hurt me." I shivered a little.

"Are you cold?" he asked as he pulled me closer to him. I could feel the heat from his body. It felt nice, reassuring in a way.

"A little," I said.

"Let's go in the bedroom, and we can get under the blanket and get you warm?"

I hesitated. He'd gone to the bedroom with my brother before, and Joe seemed fine, but I wasn't sure what was happening or what I should do.

"You trust me, don't you?"

"Yes."

He stood and pulled me up from the couch and started walking toward my bedroom. *He's an adult, and I'm supposed to do what they tell me to do*, I thought. Hesitantly, I followed.

He opened my door and walked in. I reached for the light, but he put his hand on mine. "We don't need the light. Let's just lay down and talk."

He led me to the bed and pulled the covers back. He slipped his shoes off. He nodded, and I got in bed. He lay down next to me and pulled me close. I could see moonlight filtering through the windows, casting shadows across the room, shadows that seemed to come alive, watching.

"I want to show you what your girlfriend will do for you sometime. It'll feel good."

I wasn't sure what to say, and I didn't know what was going to happen, so I remained silent. My heart banged against my chest. I reminded myself that he'd done this with my brother, and Joe never said anything bad had happened.

His hand rubbed over my chest and down my stomach slowly, and then his hand was inside my pants, squeezing through my underwear. I shivered again and felt a stirring beneath his touch.

"Just relax. I promise I won't do anything you don't want me to do, and if you want me to stop, I will. Do you want me to stop?"

"I don't know," I said shakily. This felt wrong. My mind raced. He was an adult, and you were supposed to trust adults. *Well, I couldn't trust Marcella, but that was different*, I thought. Johnny wasn't hitting me or calling me names. He was nice, so I could trust him, I tried to reassure myself. My heart was thrusting against my chest, and my mind was racing.

"Give it a minute, and you'll see, okay? Trust me, Bobby." He unbuttoned my pants and slid his hand inside, rubbing and squeezing and making me harder. It felt really good, but this didn't seem right. I reminded myself he was an adult, and he knew better than I did what was right or wrong.

"Relax. It's okay." He tugged my underwear down and kept rubbing. "Do you want me to stop?"

"No, I don't think so," I whispered.

He was kissing my private. I tried pushing him away, but he kept on and held one of my wrists. I was scared and trembling, but it also felt good in a weird kind of way. I'd never had these sensations before. I wanted him to stop, but I didn't want the pleasure to stop. His mouth moved up and down. I tried to relax, but my mind ran wildly. Was *this* okay? Was this really what my girlfriend would do one day? "I...I...I think I'm going to pee."

He continued doing what he was doing.

"Wait, wait, I'm..."

Something happened. It felt like I was peeing but not the same. He rose back up and leaned in to kiss my lips. I turned away. "Has that never happened before?" Johnny asked.

"Did I pee in your mouth?"

"No, that's called an orgasm. You came. It's something guys can do, and girls like it when we do. Was that okay?" he asked. "You aren't mad at me, are you?"

"No, I just, I—"

"I'd never do anything to hurt you, Bobby. I love you, kid. It's okay. You didn't do anything wrong."

"You sure?" I asked.

"Certainly. People do this all the time, but it has to be our secret, okay? You can't tell anyone, especially your mom and dad. They wouldn't understand. Do you get it?"

"Yes." I didn't.

"I'm going to go, but I just want you to know that you can trust me, and I hope I can trust you to keep our secret."

"I will," I said hesitantly. Who could I tell about it anyway? Was there anyone I could ask if it was wrong or right? I was embarrassed. I was afraid. I was also thankful for something in my life that didn't bring me pain. I think one thing that sort of normalized what happened was that for many years, he and Joe had wrestled, and it sometimes led to the bedroom. No one ever said it was wrong, and if they did the same thing, then it must be okay. I never really knew what happened in the dark room, but now I could only imagine this is what was going on.

He left, and I lay there, wondering what happened. It did feel good. It wasn't like what Marcella did to me. He wasn't mean, and he didn't call me names like the kids at school. I didn't know whom to ask about it, but I had kind of promised to keep the secret anyway. He's a grown-up, I reminded myself.

I got out of bed and went to the bathroom, where I turned on the shower. I got in, and as the hot water pelted me, I started crying uncontrollably. "God, please help me understand," I wept.

He came back week after week. I dreaded it. I wanted the attention he gave me. He told me he loved me and how special I was to him, which were words I'd been longing to hear, but that didn't take away the nudging of guilt I felt. When he left, I got in the shower and cried again. I felt dirty, ashamed, and alone.

Some weekends when he didn't come by early, he'd come home with my parents and would lie down in my brother's old bed or on the couch. I'd hear my dad and stepmother arguing, but they'd finally go to bed. Shortly after that, Johnny would come sit on my bed. "Bobby," he'd whisper, "are you awake?"

I would not answer, trying to pretend to be asleep. He would lie down next to me and start messing with me. Things would repeat themselves. I couldn't help it. I started crying.

"If you want me to stop and not come back, I will do that. Is that what you want?"

"Yes," I said meekly, "I think so."

He always came back, though, no matter what I said. I always felt guilty, but I always gave in. I'd tell him to stop sometimes, but he'd continue as if he hadn't heard me. I couldn't tell Darla what he did because I didn't think she'd understand. Joe had already escaped and was moving on with his life. I didn't know what they'd say or think of me if they knew. I remembered what Johnny told me about no one understanding. I was afraid of being blamed or punished for what happened if someone said that it was wrong. Was it my fault? Was I bad like I imagined?

I knew I definitely couldn't go to my parents. I was already terrified of Marcella and figured she'd turn it against me somehow and make it my fault. I was scared to tell Dad, and he had already proven that he wouldn't protect me if it was wrong. I was too ashamed to tell the few friends I had because I didn't know what they'd think of me. Did this happen to them? Whom could I tell at school? A teacher? the counselor? the principal? They didn't stop the bullying that happened on a daily basis, so I didn't feel I could trust them to tell me if it was right or wrong, and if it was wrong, what would they do? Probably contact my parents, which would be something I was avoiding for good reason.

Once again, I was alone. I felt like a freak. I wished it had never started, but a part of me craved any sort of attention that wasn't violent, and *that* made me feel guilty. What could I do? Where could I turn? Whom could I trust? Did this bring me back to having to trust Johnny and what he told me?

Another thing that scratched at the back of my mind was that I always wondered about how things happened before he arrived at the house because it always seemed like remarkable timing. My parents had a phone in their bedroom. On Saturdays, they went dancing and drinking. My stepmother would be getting ready in the bedroom and then within thirty to forty-five minutes of them leaving, Johnny would arrive. I wondered if she was calling him at the bar to let him know they were leaving. Had she been preparing us for this predator the whole time? Why did no one ever ask about what I would later learn were called hickeys that were left on my neck by Johnny?

I didn't consider myself gay or straight. I don't think I even put much thought into it at that point in my life. I found women beautiful and had crushes on girls at school, although none wanted anything to do with me. But I also know that I found men handsome. It didn't seem weird to me, and I accepted that it was just a fact that some men were handsome, and some women were beautiful. I was too young to think of it as anything more than a simple observation.

As you get older you hear girls commenting on other girls appearances without it meaning they were gay, but guys just didn't talk that way about other guys. It was totally separate from a sexual thing. Johnny was my sexual awakening, and that was totally abnormal and so far from what should have happened that it had to have had some lasting effect on me as I grew older. Since girls didn't seem interested in me romantically, I never really dated, although I did go to a few dances with girls who were more friends than anything else.

There were so many wolves in my life that I, at times, just felt like giving up. I prayed about it, begging for it to stop or for answers to come. I cried out to God for help. Heaven was silent once more. Later, people would ask why I even believed in God if He did nothing to protect me. I survived and thrived one day, so I knew He *did* protect me, and He gave me salvation freely. If God watched His Son beaten and dying on the cross and could do nothing, He had possibly kept me from even worse things happening than what did.

In reading the Bible, I knew that bad things happened to good people as well as bad people and that God never promised us paradise on this side of life. I had to believe that after the beatings or abuse, He sent an angel to hold me and remind me of His love. I survived with my faith partially intact, and that was enough! Would I change everything if I could? Of course, but there's nothing you can do about your past but learn to accept it and heal from it. Sometimes, survival is enough.

Escaping the Dark Castle

> People say, "Oh, we ought to fight for animal rights."
> We fought for human rights, but even if humans have
> rights, they can still be horribly abused and are every day.
> You don't have to go to some far-off land, faraway place;
> we have a lot of child abuse in our own society.
>
> —Jane Goodall

In October of 1981, when a cousin died, unbeknownst to me and my sister, my brother called the funeral home and talked to Mom for the first time. It wasn't until December of the same year that we had Vanessa, our sister-in-law, over because of a puppy we found that needed a home, and we found the courage to ask that difficult question. "Have you or Joe found our mom yet?" we asked.

We caught her off guard, but after a minute, she nodded. "Yes, we have. It was October when Joe saw one of your cousins had died, so he called the funeral home and asked to speak to her."

We smiled. "Would she want to see us?"

"I'm sure she would love to see you," she said with a laugh. "Let me talk to your brother, and we'll get back with you soon. I promise."

She kept her promise, and we went to their house to nervously speak to Mom over the phone for the first time. I cannot express how it felt. To hear her voice again and hear the words "I love you" be spoken after so many years was incredibly moving. We laughed, we cried, and she promised that she would soon be up to see us.

I will never forget the first time I saw my mother. It was the day of my sixteenth birthday. The only picture I'd ever seen of my mother was from her high school graduation that my grandmother had saved from the fire, and I thought she looked like a movie star. I had seen pictures of her from my brother and sister-in-law, but it would not be the same as seeing her in person.

The day was going well. Early afternoon, we talked on the phone as I sat in my dad's room so I could keep an eye out the window. We agreed to meet at a grocery store nearby around four. I was so excited that I was halfway there when I realized I had left her number lying on Dad's bed and had to run back home to retrieve my evidence. My dad and Marcella thought I was at work, and I prayed they didn't call or check on me.

Mom told me she was in a brown Volare station wagon. I turned the corner, and my heart leapt out of my chest as I saw a black-haired woman barely visible over the steering wheel, sitting at the curb. She was the most beautiful person I think I had ever laid eyes on. I opened the car door and croaked, "Mom?"

"Son," Mom smiled, "get in, and let's get on with our night. Happy birthday, son!"

I grinned at her from the passenger seat and just stared at her, amazed by her beauty and the reality that she was sitting here beside me.

We drove to Mustang and drank Cokes at Del Rancho. She offered a meal, but though I had not eaten, I was too nervous and excited that food was the last thing I wanted. We talked for hours, and it was as if we'd never been apart. She was so easy to talk to.

"Would you like to see your grandmother?" she asked.

"Yes," I answered excitedly.

"She lives right here in town just a little ways from here."

We drove to her house, and I went in and was welcomed into the arms of my grandmother. We spent another few hours just talking.

The time finally came when it had to end, and she drove me back home. She dropped me off a couple blocks from the house. "We'll stay in touch," she promised. "You can call me anytime, and whenever I'm up, we'll get together. I love you so much, son, and I had a great time with you tonight. I hope you had a good birthday!"

"Thanks for the best birthday gift ever," I grinned.

We hugged, and I reluctantly went out into the night, which suddenly felt colder than before. I walked home feeling like I was on top of the world. My heart was full, and I felt complete for once. It was hard walking away from the happiness I'd just shared with my mom knowing what I was walking back into. I just kept my head down, focused on school, and dreamed of the life I might have had if only my mom could have taken me the night she left my dad.

Then in April of 1982, the incident with my dad that led to us moving in with my brother happened. Once school was out, Mom and Henry agreed to bring us to their home in East Texas. Before we left for the trip to my new home, we stopped at Henry's sister's house, and I got to meet more of his family. It was a great time, and I was looking through her stack of games when I came across a Ouija board. I'd seen them in movies but had never actually seen one in real life.

I asked one of my cousins about it, and he said it was pretty cool. They carried it into the living room, and a few of them gathered around to play with it. I was fascinated to see it moving but assumed one of them was pushing it to spell out things.

When we left, my aunt said I could take it with me if I wanted to. I knew nothing about any rules or how it worked, but I sat in the back seat with it and would quietly ask it questions, and it would sometimes move. Since I was the only one with my fingers on it, I became enthralled with it actually working.

As we traveled to Mom's home, Henry stopped the station wagon at the beginning of the bridge that crossed from Oklahoma into Texas. He told me, "You have to get out and cross the bridge."

"What?" I asked, thinking he was kidding.

He explained if he crossed the state line with me, it could be considered kidnapping, but if I walked freely over the border, it wouldn't be. My sister had graduated, so she didn't have to. It felt good, though. As I walked, I thought of all the abuse I had been through with Marcella and Johnny and imagined it all falling off in the breeze. This could be my new beginning, chapter 1 to this part of my life.

It was a different world. Henry and Mom fought sometimes, but it wasn't the same screaming, cussing, throwing things, or physical violence. They argued like what I imagined normal people did. They also drank sometimes, but it wasn't the same crazy drunkenness I'd grown up with. They both smoked as well, but it wasn't layers of smoke in the house with yellowed walls, and they'd crack the window if they smoked in the car. A few months in, I sat in my mom's lap and asked her to please quit smoking because I wanted her for many years to come. She said she'd try and put the cigarettes down and never picked them up again. This meant the world to me.

I spent hours with the Ouija board, playing it alone because everyone else refused to do it with me. This would become somewhat of an infatuation with me trying to understand how it worked. I knew if I asked it questions, it would move to spell out answers, but since the Internet wasn't available at that time, I had no way to verify if there was ever any truth in what it was saying. I didn't know if it was my own mind willing it to move without my physically knowing I was doing it, or if I was speaking to actual spirits.

It seemed harmless and was entertaining until one day late that summer, when as I asked it questions, it seemed to feel different. When I asked whom I was speaking to, it began to spell S-A-T-A. I took my fingers off and began to shake. I thought for a minute and then said, "If this is really you, then show me by knocking on the door or something."

After a few seconds, I realized what I had just said and became terrified. I knew that if someone knocked on the door at that exact moment, regardless of what it was, I would jump out of my skin. I set the board aside and fell to my knees, begging God for forgiveness and promising to put it away and never use it again if He'd keep me safe. I placed it back in the box and shoved it under my bed. I never thought about it again for quite some time.

Soon after moving to Ore City, Texas, I got a job at Catfish Village as a dishwasher, and my mom would drive me back and forth. It was a small town, so there were not many options, but this was one of the biggest restaurants in the area, and I would learn that people from Dallas, Texarkana, and many other far-off locations would travel to eat there.

I focused on being the best dishwasher and busser I could be and learned everything I could. It didn't take long until I was promoted to prep and cook. I loved learning, and though there was a lot to do, I made a friend with one of the other cooks who was around my age, and we had a lot of fun together. I saved every cent I could. My mom and Henry weren't rich, so I tried to help with school supplies and clothes, but I did still save a lot of money. It felt good to see money in the bank and have the opportunity to buy things for my family on the holidays. I was praised for my hard work, and it felt like I had finally found something I could do well.

We spent the rest of the summer going on many family day trips to different places in between my work schedule. It was a whole new way of life for me. I enjoyed the laughter and time we spent together. I didn't totally forget my life before, but the pain of it began to fade with each day I was away. Mom helped me feel normal, loved, and wanted.

When my brother and sister were in, we all played with my mom, having water fights or wrestling, as if we were kids again. This didn't bode well with Henry as he soon grew tired of all the horseplay, but it did little to slow us down. Was this what I had missed my entire childhood? It felt so unfair. At one point, Henry became so disgruntled, he bought a bus ticket and was planning on leaving, but Mom talked him back home, and we at least tried to grow out of our lost childhood and play less.

I also loved my job. On weekends, David Beard, the owner, worked side by side with me, telling me how he had a dream and decided to go after it. He started with a little building and brought truckloads of catfish in, where it was cleaned, cut, breaded, and fried for eager customers. The business grew over time and became so popular, he moved into a larger building and then built the place where I worked with two cook lines, three dining rooms, and a private bar with its own tables. Most nights, I had the job of keeping four double fryers filled with baskets of golden-fried fish, steak fries, and hot-water corn bread hush puppies. On weekends, the second line opened to accommodate the third larger dining room and bar.

I came in each afternoon to peel and slice potatoes, chop cabbage for coleslaw, prepare tartar and cocktail sauce, thaw boxes of catfish, and prepare our mixture of cornmeal and flour for the fish. After thawing, we had a particular way to wash the fish and did so until the water was clean. It was the best-tasting catfish I'd ever eaten, and the hush puppies were very unique. It was a dream job, and I worked without asking for additional time off because I loved it that much.

One weekend, my brother and sister-in-law were coming in, and I begged my mom to take off. I idolized my brother. He had the perfect life, a good job, nice car, nice home, and a loving wife—everything I desired for myself. Mom said I needed to work, but I still asked and was given off that Saturday.

Late that evening, I received a call from my boss, asking if I could come in on Sunday to help clean up. I kidded that they just couldn't do it without me. He quietly explained that at close, a man had come into the restaurant and approached the register with a gun. The manager's office was behind the register with a sliding glass window that allowed the manager to view what was going on in the lobby. The manager was counting the evening's earnings to prepare for the deposit when the man shoved the cashier out of the way and leapt over the counter, pointing the gun through the opening in the glass windows.

A server stood frozen in the office doorway as the manager pushed the money toward the man and told him to take the money but not hurt anyone. He shoved the gun to her throat and pulled the trigger. As she fell to the floor and the server tried to shield her with her body, the man grabbed a handful of cash and leapt back over the counter to run out the door. As he ran, he dropped cash and left with only a very small amount that seemed ridiculous at the cost of someone's life. He was eventually captured by the police and locked in the jail of a nearby town.

A few months later, as he awaited trial, we heard that he had escaped by tying sheets together and squeezing out of the window.

We were on high alert because we often left the back door open for fresh air, and behind the restaurant was mostly open woods.

One afternoon, as I cooked in the kitchen, the server who had held the manager as she died, came running in with panic and fear on her face. "He's here," she cried. "He's come back, and he's going to kill us!"

"Who's here?" we asked urgently.

"Th-the man who robbed us," she stuttered. "He's here, and he's going to kill me."

She trembled with fear as the manager carefully crept into the dining room to see what was going on. Fortunately, it wasn't he but just someone who looked similar. That experience haunted us all for many years and followed me in the back of mind throughout my career. The prisoner was arrested within a few weeks and placed in a more secure location.

I started high school in August 1982 in the small town of Ore City. I still had some bullies, and I never fully fit in to any particular group, but I made a few friends. The one thing I can say about my time in Yukon was that the education was excellent, and I was so far ahead of everyone else in English that my teacher would give me a book to read on the side, and I'd do a book report on it to keep me focused. I also became involved in journalism again and spent some time as the editor of the school newspaper, which I loved.

One day, Mom asked if I was ready for a car. Our neighbor had a '70s Chevy Vega that he sold to me for $500. I was so excited, and as far as I was concerned, it was the most beautiful car I'd ever seen. I didn't care that it wasn't new. The only thing was that it was standard, but Mom and Henry took me out each day, patiently teaching me how to drive it. I became adept enough that she let me start driving to work. We had a few moments that are hilarious now but were terrifying at the time when I struggled to get the car going again after stopping on a hill. I always prayed no one would be very close behind me because I killed and restarted it many times, sweating the entire time.

On one occasion, Mom and I had gone into Longview, the closest larger city to us to do some shopping, and as I went to leave, I got stopped on a steep incline. I groaned, and Mom just reassured me that I could do it. I begged her to switch with me to get us out safely, but she said I needed to learn it on my own. It felt like it took an hour to get out of that parking lot, but we finally made it and were able to laugh about it on the way home.

School and work flowed into one another. I'd go to school and would have about forty-five minutes to an hour before I went to work. We closed at nine, and I'd usually get home around 10:30 p.m. Sometimes I would bring leftover fish and hush puppies home with me, and we'd sit at the bar eating and talking about the day. The restaurant was closed Wednesday and Sunday, so I always had two days off to look forward to. I'd use those days to catch up on my homework.

On my break, I'd sometimes go to the nearby lake and look out at the water from my car or eat if I'd packed a lunch or picked something up. One afternoon, as I sat in my car, a man approached my open window. "How's it going?" he smiled.

"Good."

"What are you out doing this afternoon?" he asked, leaning down and putting his hands on my door. My heart leapt with fear.

"Nothing," I answered, looking around to see if there were any other cars. "I'm just killing some time before I go to work."

He stretched, and I could see his dick pressing against his tight shorts. He adjusted himself and then leaned back in, smiling. "You're really cute," he said as he reached in and grabbed my crotch.

No, no, not again. Why me? Why now? This couldn't be happening.

I fumbled with the keys and started the car and released the clutch, applying gas, and peeling away from the park, watching my rearview mirror to make sure he wasn't following. A tiny crack appeared in the door of the room that I had shoved all the memories of Johnny into, and I felt so many of the same feelings I had at that time. I did not immediately tell anyone out of fear of how they would react, but after I saw the same car in the neighborhood one afternoon, I finally told my mom. She said he was probably a pedophile and to stay away from the lake when I was by myself. I was afraid to go to the lake anymore anyway. I shoved that into the door where I had tried to lock away one of the monsters of my childhood and slammed it shut again.

Things went back to normal as the memory of what happened faded, and I got back into the routine of school, work, home to study, and sleep. Each day started over, but I loved my job, and it never got old. That, in addition to a happy homelife, made me very content for the first time in my life.

School was going well, and aside from a few people who seemed determined to make my life miserable, I enjoyed my classes and got good grades. English and journalism were my strongest, but I did well in most everything, except for PE, and I hated that. I was embarrassed changing in front of the other guys because some teased me about my big breasts. It was something I'd dealt with my whole life, so I should have been used to it, but it still hurt me deeply and just increased my insecurities and self-doubt. I had no illusions that I was ever going to be a jock or excel in sports. I just struggled to do the minimum I had to and keep myself as hidden as possible from the jeers and taunts. However, it was never as bad as what I experienced in my schools in Yukon.

In October of my senior year, we decided to try to raise some money by having a haunted house. There was an abandoned old house in town, and someone knew the right person who would let us use that, and it did indeed look the part. In our spare time, we worked on decorations and discussed how exactly we would make it work.

On one evening, as it got darker, a few started saying we should have a séance, and for whatever insane reason, I told them I had a Ouija board if they wanted to use it. They did, and so I went home and brought it back with me. We lit candles, and some of the kids gathered around the board, placing their fingers on the planchette, asking questions. I don't remember anything remarkable happening, but it did gather my interest once more.

One of the friends was Barbara, who lived about a quarter mile from where I did, and we had become friends. We talked about the Ouija board and séance that happened after the haunted house, and

I shared my experiences with her from when I first tried using it. We decided we'd try it again but bring a Christian perspective to it. She lived with her grandmother, who was elderly, so we had to be quiet. We'd meet in her room, and for the most part, we'd ask questions with my fingers on the planchette, and she'd write the questions and responses in a notebook for reference. We always started with a prayer and asked for only *good* spirits to communicate with us. Once again, I didn't know how it worked or whom we were really talking to, if anyone, but the planchette did seem to move on its own, and though it sometimes moved slowly and methodically, there were times when it was going so fast, I could barely keep my fingers on it.

We also shared a friend, Jan, who had told us she was a white witch. I didn't know much about witchcraft but assumed that was a lighter side of magic meant to do good rather than dark magic, which might be more menacing. Jan had warned us about using the Ouija board because she said that we did not really understand what we were messing with. We ignored her warning, although we also did not discuss anything we learned while using it.

A month or so passed, and we truly felt we were not doing any harm. Most of what was discussed was nothing of any importance, but one night, that changed. It was a school night, and at some point, the air in the room seemed to change, and the messages became darker. Amidst the messages, it spelled out something ominous—B-E-W-A-R-E-O-F-J-A-N.

The planchette chose the letters as I spoke them aloud for Barbara to write down. I looked at her, and she looked at me with the same bewilderment.

I asked why we should beware of Jan, and it just spelled out the same warning a couple more times. I took my fingers off and took a deep breath.

It didn't seem to be spelling out much of anything, and then it acted as if it had a life of its own. It raced around the board, pausing briefly at each letter, and I could barely keep my fingers on the plastic piece with the clear window.

After a few more minutes of this, I asked whom I was speaking to, and it spelled out A-N-T-I-C-H-R-I-S-T. I laughed aloud, though a part of me felt a chill run through my body. I asked for the name, and it spelled out a man's name. I asked where he was, and it gave us the name of a town I was unfamiliar with. Then it paused and spelled out another name and then another name. This went on for several times before it finally spelled out the name Paris, which I knew there was a place in Texas with that name. It spelled another and another, as if it were moving. Some of the towns we both recognized as places in Texas.

Then it spelled out a name that gave us both a start—Ore City. I yanked my fingers away and looked at Barbara to see if she felt the same terror I did. "This is weird," I mumbled as I pushed the board away from me. "It's as if it were traveling. Is that even possible?"

"I have no idea, but I don't want to do any more tonight," Barbara said firmly.

"Me either," I agreed and began gathering my things.

It was close to nine, and we said very little else as I walked out into the night. It wasn't a long walk home, but it was dark, and the dirt road was not well lit. It seemed like an endless journey to get to the house, and my mind raced over and over what had just happened. I was never so thankful as to see the lights on in the living room as I walked in. My mom asked if I had a good time, and I mumbled a reply and then told her I was going to bed.

I knelt beside the bed and prayed for protection from any forces that would mean to do us any harm. I could not forget the image of the planchette racing around and the words it spelled out. It felt very menacing. It felt like forever before sleep overtook me.

I rode the bus to school the next morning, saying very little to anyone. I got off the bus and was heading to my first class when Jan approached me. "Were you playing the Ouija board last night?" she asked.

"No," I lied, though my face was probably whiter than snow.

"I told you to be careful, that you didn't know what you were messing with. Did it say something about me?"

"No. Seriously, we didn't use the Ouija board last night. I'm going to be late to my class."

I turned and walked away, feeling as if ice was growing within me, trying to consume me.

After first period ended, I went searching for Barbara, thinking she had somehow contacted Jan the night before, and they were playing a trick on me. I saw her face in the crowd, but as I neared her and before I could say anything, she asked me a question. "Did you tell Jan what happened last night?" she seemed to be staring into my soul.

"Why do you ask?" I questioned.

"Because she said some weird things about us using the Ouija board last night, and I figured you must have told her something."

This was long before cell phones or emails, and I found it unlikely that Barbara's grandmother would have let her use the phone that late at night, but I simply couldn't believe that this could be real. Barbara never said she was playing a trick on me either.

When I got home that evening, I read through the words that Barbara had written and I had spelled out in the notebook. I once again prayed for forgiveness if I had tampered with something I did not fully understand or wasn't meant to be messing with.

That weekend, I took the Ouija board out to the burn barrel and covered it with lighter fluid and placed newspaper around it and set it on fire. I watched it burn for a while and then went back in the house, swearing to never touch a Ouija board again. It might have been no more than a joke played on me, but no one ever said differently, and I never talked about it again to any of them. Lesson learned.

The rest of the year was fairly uneventful and continued with the rotation of school, work, home, and sleep. I appreciated whatever *normal* routines I could invite into my life. School passed quickly enough, and in spring of 1984, I graduated. The last two years of my life, with a few exceptions, had been a blessing, and I gained a small amount of confidence in myself. I was still socially awkward in crowds due to low self-esteem, and I had only a handful of people I would call friends, but I had made it to the end of school.

Once graduation was over, I began trying to decide what to do with the rest of my life. I really wanted to go to college to become a psychologist so I could help people who struggled with many of the problems I had. I also enjoyed journalism and writing, so I wondered about becoming a reporter but was afraid my lack of self-confidence would stand in my way of being successful. I had left my past as behind as I could, but the effects of all the emotional, physical, verbal, and sexual abuse had established its place in my life. It affected my lack of self-worth and confidence that I was able to accomplish anything on my own.

Henry had been in the military and felt like I should go that route and that it would open up opportunities for college and a career after I got out. I really had to wrestle with my demons and push to make a decision, but I really had no idea where to begin, so I eventually conceded to visit the recruiter in Longview. I met with one, took some tests, and settled on becoming a security specialist with the air force. I still had so many doubts as to whether I could do it or not but felt my choices were slipping away, and I had to make a decision. I was accepted into the air force and pushed forward with that option.

I completed my physical, filled out my paperwork, and waited. I received my boot camp instructions to start in October of 1984.

I arrived with excitement and a little bit of nerves, but since the recruiters had been so nice, I didn't anticipate any problems. I was skinny but not really in shape, so the anticipation of what the physical requirements would be did make me nervous. I took a bus to Shreveport, Louisiana, and then we were driven to the airport. I had never flown before, so this would be a new experience for me, and it added to my anxiety.

We safely arrived in San Antonio, and a few of us waited together for the bus that would continue to the Lackland Air Force Base to arrive. I remember most that the people in charge were kind of rude by the time we got to the airport, and I thought that I'd remember that if we had a chance of rating them later on. At the air force base, we were taken to the area of our flight where the basic training took place, and we lined up slowly in the dark. I was handed papers for the recruits that I was to hand over to the sergeant. I was ready for bed. It had been a long day.

"Everyone needs to stand up and keep their mouths shut until your sergeant arrives," a uniformed man ordered us.

We stood for what felt like hours, and a few of the people disregarded the previous order and sat on their bags, and others were talking amongst themselves. I had slacks, a dress shirt, and loafers that were killing my feet, but I kept standing.

Suddenly, a door slammed open, and a tiny man came stomping out. He was small in stature but not in spirit. "Stand up!" he shouted. "I don't want to hear a word out of anyone!" Though he was small, he certainly wasn't meek at all, and his voice boomed through the patio area where we stood.

"Okay," he continued, "everyone pick up your bags!"

We picked our bags up in varying speeds. I juggled the papers and my bag.

"Put them down!" he screamed.

Seriously? I thought.

"Now pick up your bags," he ordered.

We did a little better and were slightly faster this time.

"Put your bags down!" he screamed again.

We did so grudgingly.

"Now, pick up your bags and be quick about it!"

I did so, praying I would not drop the papers as they shuffled a little in my hands. I was in the front row toward the end, and our sergeant started walking down the line of guys, stopping to stare at a few and make comments about hippy hair, bad attitudes, or sloppy clothes. By the time he made it to me, I was sweating, and my knees felt like they were going to give out.

"Well, aren't you pretty in your slacks and shirt," he smiled. "I guess you think you're going to get special treatment because you've got that slick haircut?"

I assumed he wasn't really *talking* to me, so I kept my mouth shut. Fortunately, he continued down the line. He ordered us to carry our bags up the stairs to our next destination. We entered a large room filled with beds, some filled with bodies and some empty. He directed us to drop our bags against the wall and pull out a pen.

We did as told. He then lined us up. I was nestled against a stack of jackets at the end. "Sit down!" he yelled.

We did.

"Stand up!" he screamed.

Seriously, again?

"When I tell you to do something, I need you to get the lead out and do it!

"Sit down!

"Stand up!"

Every time I stood and went down, my arm brushed the jackets, and I could feel a few of them sliding toward me. I quietly prayed they wouldn't fall and tried to push them back up with my right hand.

"Sit down!"

I guess we satisfied him because he finally stopped.

He handed out a stack of books and had us pass them down. Once they were passed out, he told us to pull our pens out. Shit. Mine had been in my hand when I was pushing the jackets back up. He started telling us things to write down. I whispered to the guy next to me to see if he had a pen I could use. We traded back and forth. It didn't really matter because we would laugh later that no one could really read what we wrote because our nerves were shot. He talked for a time and then had us pick up our bags and go to find an empty bed. We were learning and tried to move faster.

Once we stood at the foot of our beds I took the time to look around. None of the people who arrived earlier were moving in their beds. Smart. He directed us to put our bags in the lockers and then used a padlock to lock them in. The padlock had a set of keys that we were to put around our necks. I placed mine around my neck and then tried to pull it from the padlock, but it wouldn't budge.

By now, our sergeant had been joined by another, and I could hear them pacing down the walkway and talking. I started sweating again, cold with fear at not being able to get my key free. I heard someone walk up behind me and thought I was going to pass out from stress.

"Are you an idiot?" my sergeant asked. "Do you not know how a lock works?" He grabbed my chain and pushed the padlock closed and then pulled the key out.

Yes, I am an idiot, I thought. My nerves were shot that first day!

I lay in bed that night and thought back on the night. I decided the smartest thing to do was to shut up, keep my eyes down, and do everything that I was ordered to do. It didn't take long to figure out why we marched for hours in what appeared to be circles with heavy backpacks. I felt it was meant to help us get in shape. Underwear was ironed in a six-inch square, which seemed kind of stupid, but you had to learn to follow orders. We had to drink two eight-ounce glasses of water before we ate, and I knew that was to fill us up and hydrate us. The food was delicious and plentiful, but the first two weeks, we weren't allowed to partake in dessert, including the ice cream freezers full of icy delights, cleansing us of sugar. I gained ten pounds but lost inches. I was the smallest and fittest I'd ever been. I even got used to the yelling because I told myself that if we were in war, people would be screaming amidst chaos, so if we couldn't handle it now, how could we be ready for it in battle? An idiot? Not completely!

Graduation came, and the final obstacle course that I would have never been able to do six weeks prior was relatively easy for me. Some of my family came for the special event, and I was really proud of my achievement. There wasn't much of a break in between basic and tech school, but my security-specialist training was still at Lackland, so I didn't have to do a lot of traveling.

The first two weeks of tech school, we weren't allowed to leave the base, so we separated into fours and went into people's homes for Thanksgiving. It was a great experience. Our family had Penn-Dutch heritage, and the food was incredibly good. We came back, worked hard, and looked forward to Christmas break. I had never shot a gun, but I was in the top of my class for marksmanship. I had pretty much straight As, so life was good.

Right before we left for Christmas break, I was told I'd been selected with forty-nine others to participate in a special program once we graduated, which would give me specialized training and access to every base in the world. Of course, I accepted the offer, then I went home to my family for the holidays. Life was perfect!

It was good to be away from all the studying and hard work and just relax. There was a lot of joy and laughter as I stayed with Mom, and I had gifts for everyone underneath the tree. One night, after everyone had gone to bed, I was sitting in the floor by my mom as we talked about so many things. She shocked me with one question. "Son," she said quietly, "your brother told us a few weeks ago that Johnny had sexually assaulted him when he lived at home with your dad, and we wondered if anything happened to you?"

The air was sucked out of the room. I felt ice crawling into my veins. I stared at her for a minute, trying to digest what she had told me. My heart felt like it was going to beat out of my chest, and I felt my face flush with shame. What do I say? I had tried to block those memories, forget them. They were locked away safely. The crack in the door widened.

"I don't...," I started, and then I fell into her lap wracked with tears. Everything seemed to explode around me.

Mom held me and told me she loved me no matter what. I could not speak for a long time.

"So," I sniffled, "when Joe moved out, Johnny started on me? I'm so embarrassed. I'm sorry." I felt as if I was being pulled into an ocean of darkness.

"Son, it's not your fault. You were an innocent child, and that son of a bitch took advantage of you! You had so much else to deal with, and I'm sorry that you had to deal with this too. I just wish you had felt like you could tell me."

"Tell you?" I questioned. "I couldn't tell anyone. I tried to forget it when I moved out. I locked it in a room, and though I'd think of it at times, I tried to tell myself it wasn't real. I wanted to believe it didn't really happen."

"Well," my mom consoled me, "it did, and we are going to tell your dad and call the police. He won't get away with this."

It was a long way back to Lackland Air Force Base, and the closer we got, the colder it became. By the time we made it to my dormitory, it had started snowing, blanketing everything around me.

It was the first snow they'd had in a hundred years and almost completely shut down the city of San Antonio. It fit my mood. I was shutting down as well.

My grades began to suffer, and my As turned into Ds and Fs. I couldn't concentrate. I couldn't remember what I studied anymore. If this wasn't enough, I got notice that my grandmother was dying, and my stepdad was going to have open-heart surgery. I told my roommate one afternoon that I felt like my life was spinning out of control, and I just wanted to die.

The next day, my sergeant pulled me aside and asked what was going on. I looked him in the eyes and burst into tears. When I calmed down, I quietly told him what had happened over the holiday and the news I'd just received. He recommended counseling.

Reluctantly, I did go and tried to be open to sharing about the abuse that had occurred in my early life. After several meetings, the counselor recommended that I go home and find closure, and then I could return with a few weeks of basic and complete my tech-school training. I got it. Here's a kid very messed up, so who wanted to put a gun in his hands?

The discharge took long enough that I was still on the base when my flight graduated. I didn't have the heart to go. Once again, I had failed. Marcella had been right. I couldn't do anything right.

When I arrived back at my mom's house, she met me with a hug and told me she loved me, but I could see the disappointment in her eyes. I felt it too. We talked for a while, and she told me that my brother had told our dad, and then they had gone to the police. The police had pulled Johhny in for questioning, and he eventually confessed about me, my brother, and thirteen other boys. It was a taped confession. His hand was slapped, and he was ordered to get counseling. I was furious!

"No jail?" I cried incredulously. "And *he* gets counseling? What about the fifteen boys he molested?"

"Son, I agree. It's not right, and we are all mad. We just have to get you through this, and I pray he pays in his own way!"

I felt like laughing at that. Prayers weren't heard. God wasn't listening. Someone could destroy lives and get away with it? Was this justice? My life, my dreams for something better, my hope that the past was the past were dashed against the rocks of futility. I just wanted to feel normal, but I had received a reminder that my life was nothing but that and would always be something that was very much the opposite.

A Broken Toy

> Child abuse is one of those issues that's very difficult to talk about because it's surrounded by guilt and shame and so on, but us avoiding that issue doesn't help those kids in need out there who need support.
>
> —Chris Hemsworth

I had to be out of the air force for six months before I could reapply, so I started searching for work. One afternoon, I ran into the owner of the catfish restaurant where I worked during high school, and he asked what I was doing. I left out the military and just said I was trying to figure out what to do with my life. "Would you be interested in coming back to work with me?" he asked. "We are opening a new restaurant in Kilgore, Texas, and I'd love if you came on as a manager. You always did a great job and gave me everything you had."

I was stunned at the offer but accepted. I started work as an assistant manager at the brand-new restaurant and was excited to see it all through fresh eyes. I knew it as a cook but never saw the parts of management, so this was exhilarating and filled me with a new vitality that helped erase the wounds of the past.

Catfish King is where I met Susan, the woman I would eventually marry. I was trying to fill a void in my life. I was grasping for the life my brother and sister had. I wanted that good job, a house, wife, kids, and church that I felt was lacking. We worked together, and though she was a few years younger than me, she had a laugh that drew me to her. We would talk as we portioned cups of tartar sauce. She helped me feel normal.

On Easter, she came in with her hair and makeup done and had a yellow dress that lit up her face. I was perplexed when she smiled at me. Me? Was it possible that she liked me? Could anyone like me?

We started dating, and though I felt awkward and my past clawed at the doors of my memories, I held to the belief that I could have a normal life with someone who could love me. As the months passed, we grew closer. I wanted to believe it was love. I cared about her, thought about her when we weren't together, felt relaxed and comfortable with her. We kissed and made out, but I was insistent that I didn't want to have sex until marriage. I was too ashamed to admit that the thought terrified me.

We talked about getting married, so one day, I asked her father if he'd allow me to marry her. He insisted we wait until she'd graduated, but we were convinced we had to be married right then. He finally relented, saying if we'd elope, in ten years, he'd pay for her to have the wedding she dreamed of. She didn't want to elope, and she didn't want to wait, and I wanted her to have whatever she wanted. I had saved money, so I told her we could plan a small wedding. I was afraid if we waited, she'd decide she didn't want to be with me anymore. No one had ever wanted me, and I didn't want to lose this chance. I tried to give her as perfect of a day as I could afford and didn't think twice about reaching into all the money I'd saved over the years.

We got married in October of 1985. I wanted my family to be a part of it, but they all felt like I was rushing things and making a mistake. My brother and sister didn't attend the wedding, and that broke my heart. I loved them both so much and wanted them to share in my happiness. I had been at both of their weddings, so I felt rejected by those I loved the most. My mom did come, albeit with hesitation, and that was good enough for me. The wedding was easy, but the wedding night and honeymoon were a nightmare.

I'd never been all the way with a girl before, so I was clueless and unsure of myself. I felt awkward and terrified that I would not be able to satisfy Susan. What if we had sex, and she hated it? What if she decided she did not want to be with me because I was not a good lover? All I knew about making love was from the movies or books I had read, and they did not provide step-by-step instructions.

Our wedding night became a reality, and we retired to the suite her mom had given us as a wedding present. We had a huge Jacuzzi in our bathroom, so we decide to relax in there first. I was nervous and excited as we undressed and sank into hot, bubbling water. We kissed and explored one another in the water.

As we dried off and started toward the bed, I became more and more anxious. Susan told me to relax as we crawled in under the covers. I tried to fall into the moment, but every time I closed my eyes, I saw Johnny leering at me. He had come with me on my wedding night. Could I never be free from him?

We tried, but I wasn't able to perform. I didn't know what to say or if I should say anything. I reassured her that I was just nervous, and it meant nothing about how I felt about her. I asked her to be patient, and she was.

We drove to Oklahoma and stayed in a cabin that my stepdad's family owned. Everything was perfect until it came to sex. We lay on a bed in front of a fire, holding one another. There was not anything more romantic, but I could not escape Johnny. I could not relax or enjoy the moment. Our honeymoon ended, and Susan confided in my mom that I was having trouble. My mom shared some of what had happened and asked her to be patient. She was patient, but I felt damaged. It took time, but we finally were able to be intimate.

We had an apartment in Kilgore, Texas. I tried to make up for my lack in the bedroom by giving her everything I could. That Christmas, I filled our living room with gifts for her. I loved her and wanted her to feel loved but was too naive to realize gifts did not replace passion.

For a while, life was relatively good, and I thought I might have that life I dreamed of. I can remember holding her as she would sing to me as I drifted into sleep. It seemed perfect.

Susan was still a high schooler at heart and was trying to live that life while I wanted her focus on me and our relationship. It caused tension that grew over time. I was jealous of the guys who came over when I was at work. She insisted they were just friends, but something scratched at old wounds, and I drowned in my insecurities.

While dating we had begun attending a Baptist church in Kilgore. We had been invited by our coworker and my best man, Kenny. His brother was pastor of the church. This was the church we were married in. Church was new to me, and I absorbed everything like a sponge. The church was an Independent Fundamental Baptist church that taught women wore dresses and men wore short hair.

They believed firmly in the King James Version of the Bible, which was something different for me. It felt like a foreign language at first, but as I studied the Scriptures, I became more familiar with the speech. I found it funny today that upon investigation, King James allegedly had both male lovers and female mistresses.

The short hair was fine, but wearing only dresses was a change for Susan, and we fought over this many a day. For me, it was all or nothing. If we were going to be a part of the church, we had to do everything it taught. I ripped shorts to keep her from wearing them and threw away earrings that were too secular to be wearing in such a conservative environment. I would later look back with shame that I was that person, but I was struggling to awaken the Christian side of myself, and since I had never attended church, what I was hearing preached from the pulpit was the only truth I knew. In my mind, I was being the kind of man that God expected me to be by holding my wife accountable to uphold His standards.

I fought to be the head of the home, which was what we were taught in church, but since my personality was less dominant than Susan's, conflict arose at every turn. I overcompensated by demanding compliance, and it was lost on me that I was becoming just like the ones I hated and feared growing up. In a way, I think Susan became symbolic of Marcella to me. I could not win back then, but I was determined not to lose this time. I projected all my anger and frustration on her. What started out as small fights built over time. Arguments became fights, and fights became battles, and battles led to war. But occasionally, light broke through enough to give me some semblance of hope.

In December of 1986, we found out Susan was pregnant, and we were overjoyed. She loved the attention it brought her and truly seemed to enjoy her pregnancy. The baby was likely conceived in Hot Springs, Arkansas, where we both worked at a Catfish King buffet.

We moved back to Kilgore after a few months and found a cute one-bedroom apartment. I got a job as a manager at Wendy's and started at one of their older locations in Longview, Texas. I was perplexed by a smell that I attributed to its being an older building, but one day, as I was cleaning under the salad bar, I was horrified to find that the drain was filled with maggots in all the food debris that had obviously not been cleaned in a very long time. It took several employees to get it cleaned. I did everything I could to make it a cleaner and better restaurant than I found. There was a newer Wendy's as well, and they eventually closed the one I was working at, and I was transferred to the other one. We had several extra managers since it was basically two stores in one.

Susan's pregnancy was progressing perfectly, and we were excited to be having our first child. One morning early in her pregnancy, she rolled over me in bed to answer the phone and laughed that the old wives' tales said that meant she transferred her pregnancy to me. It must have been somewhat true because I craved right along with her and gained over forty pounds. Together, we shared a lot of Frostys, triple cheeseburgers, apple dumplings, and stuffed baked potatoes.

We still fought at times, but we had moments of peace as well. At this point, most of our fights were rooted in money. We got behind on our car payments that her dad had cosigned with us, and not knowing there were options, we ended up having our new Chevy Nova repossessed. Eventually, her mom helped us get into a small car that was certainly not as nice, but it ran. Before we got it, I was having to walk several miles to and from work but spent that time praying for our relationship and our baby.

Our son was born two weeks early in August of 1987. They induced her, and as she lay struggling with labor pains, I suffered from stomach pains myself. I joked that I was fine gaining weight and having labor pains, but she was going to have the baby!

As the day progressed, she was struggling, so they recommended a C-section. They asked if I wanted to be in the room with her, and I said yes. I sat with her at the head of the table and cautiously watched the procedure. I was afraid the blood would freak me out, but as I watched them work, I became fascinated. When I saw his head, my eyes clouded with tears of joy. Our son was born! We named him Adam because he was our first, like the first man in the Bible. The moment I saw him, a part of me came alive. He was the most beautiful thing I had ever laid my eyes on. I loved him so much and believed he would be the glue that put our marriage back together.

Her parents were there with us, and while she and the baby rested, they took me to dinner at Denny's. I mostly remember my head throbbing but also appreciated the warmth and acceptance they offered me. They pledged their support and offered to help in any way they could. We were first-time parents, so we had to learn as we went, accepting advice from friends and family but learning many things the hard way. I held my son and would whisper that I would always be there for him. I would always protect him and never let anyone hurt him like I'd been hurt.

Shortly after the birth of Adam, I went in to work one morning and was told I was being let go. It was a moment of total panic, and I had no idea what to do. I wanted to run and just get away so I could clear my head. We loaded the car with a suitcase and tucked our son in the car seat and headed to Oklahoma to spend some time with family.

As the night set in and we drove into Oklahoma, I noticed the lights were getting dimmer. We were on a stretch of road with not much around, so when the car eventually died, we just stared at each other, not knowing what to do. It was a cool evening, and I told her I'd walk to the nearest town or house and see if I could call someone. She didn't want to be left in the car alone with a baby, so we wrapped Adam up as warmly as we could, said a prayer of protection, and set out into the night.

We hadn't gone far when a truck pulled up beside us and asked if we needed help. We explained our car was dead, and they offered for us to come to their house, and we'd try to come up with a plan.

They seemed safe enough, and the warmth tugging at us from inside the truck gave us enough security to say okay. I silently prayed we'd be safe. We got to their nearby farmhouse, and friendly faces invited us inside.

As we told them what we were doing and what happened to the car, they listened intently. I asked them if I could call my dad, and they gave me the phone. As I explained the situation to him and told them the people's name, he laughed and said they were distant relatives of ours. He spoke to them, and they agreed to allow us to sleep there that night, and Dad would come up the next morning and help get the car going. I smiled as I thanked God for an answer to prayer. What were the chances?

It ended up being the alternator, and my uncle had a shop, so he was able to put a new one on for us once we got to the city. I still had no idea what we were going to do, and following the advice of my dad one morning over coffee, I began looking at jobs. I did a few interviews and then found an ad for a manager at Denny's. I interviewed and was offered the job.

We relocated to Oklahoma City, and I began my training. It was one of the best training experiences I'd ever gone through, and I excelled at all my tasks. I applied all I had learned from David Beard and expanded my knowledge with an open mind. After training, I went to a Denny's on the south side of the city, and for extra money, Susan was waitressing at the Denny's where I had trained. We still struggled financially, and things weren't perfect at home, but we worked well together and remained professional. We found an Independent Baptist church in the city as well. For a while, things seemed pretty normal.

The first time I could prove she cheated was in 1988. Her parents and aunt came by the house to see Adam and felt tension in the air. After a short visit, her parents felt unwelcome, so they got up to leave. She followed them to their car and finally confided that she needed to talk to them about something. She went to her aunt's house and told them that a man at work had been calling the house and was trying to get her to go out with him, although he knew she was married. She was afraid that he was going to call her while they were there, and that was why she was so nervous. He had followed her to her car and kissed her, and she was afraid someone from work was going to tell me. She said she had been resisting doing anything else.

"You need to tell Robert what's going on," they told her.

She eventually did. After a long night of arguing, she told me that she had never loved me and that she only married me to get away from her parents. We would return to this topic over the next few years. Even with this, we were blessed with a son, and because of that, I felt we needed to remain together. We tried to put on the facade that we loved one another and were happy, but at home, we were both miserable. My son was my only source of joy. I was butting heads with my boss, who didn't like me making changes to her restaurant although they were what our district manager had directed me to do.

One night, after I sent an employee home, who had come in not in the proper uniform, my manager showed up in the middle of the rush, and I was in the server station between two of the dining rooms. She pointed her long manicured nail in my face and told me to never send *her* employees home. It was so busy, and I was furious with her. I told her I was currently taking care of business, and if her employees came in not in proper uniform on my shift, they were going to be sent home. I then told her to never stick her finger in my face again, and I turned to take care of the customers in the restaurant.

That was the beginning of the end. With the stress of what I had been told by Susan and not feeling like I was being supported at work, I decided I could not continue. I wanted to start Bible college in a church in Longview, although I knew it would not be easy. I felt I needed a change, and my focus was on my faith. We finally agreed to move back to Longview, Texas, and try to start over with our relationship. My last day, the manager who had made my life hell handed me a Bible and wished me nothing but success. I was no longer a threat to her employees.

We moved back to Texas and became as active in church as we could. I eventually did start going to school at their Bible college. My goal was to eventually get into psychology and become a counselor. I finished one semester.

One night, as we lay in bed, she started asking me if I ever thought of men. She admitted she had experimented a little with some of her girlfriends in school. I told her I found men attractive as well as women beautiful but had not explored beyond that. She hinted that maybe we should explore our own things and could still stay together for our son. I knew this was not right. I thought back to her words of never loving me. I was used to rejection but could not bear thinking our marriage was over.

We pushed on, and the path became murky, which surprised me even more when she discovered she was pregnant again in 1988. We would soon discover it was twins. For a while, the tension lifted some, and I wanted to believe things would be okay. We worked together for quite a while, and coworkers would say how they hoped they would have what we did one day. Inside, I thought if they only knew the truth! It was an illusion, but it helped me convince myself that things were fine.

In May of 1989, Susan gave birth to twin girls, Catherine and Courtney. What could be better than a beautiful daughter but two! They were delivered C-section as well, and I got to be present to cut the umbilical cords again. I was a proud father three times over. They were beautiful and healthy girls—daddy's girls! As wonderful as it was having three healthy children, it was not enough to fix the many other problems we had in our relationship.

There was a choirboy who was also a part of the Bible college, and Susan commented on how he reminded her of her father when he was young. I didn't think anything of it and focused on building on myself. I wanted to be a good father and a good husband. I wanted a good marriage. I prayed for it. I believed it would happen. Things would seem better for a moment and then would explode again.

I began admitting my struggles with depression and sought treatment. I tried some counseling but never found anyone I trusted enough to truly open up about anything to initiate any sort of real healing. I was afraid to confide in anyone about the truth of my past for fear of judgment or condemnation, and I fought hard to keep the doors closed to so much of my past that I was afraid to crack them open even a little bit.

Susan's infatuation with the guy in church was growing. I began having questions, but she always denied that anything was going on. Anytime I questioned her faithfulness, she would turn it back on me as my insecurities and lack of trust in her. I didn't know what to believe anymore or whom I could turn to see if my mistrust was without cause or not.

We were getting calls at the house, and if I answered, they would hang up. This went on for several months and would happen as often as seven to eight times per day. This eventually led to a confrontation on the day before my birthday in 1990. I came right out and asked her if she was having an affair. She finally confessed that she had been having an affair with Jeff, the choirboy she had been infatuated with. She explained it went beyond an affair, and they were in love with one another.

After a long argument, she called him at work and, around midnight, left in our car with no explanation. I reached out to her parents and told them what was happening. Around 2:00 a.m., she dropped the car off and got in Jeff's, and they drove off into the night. She didn't show back up until 11:00 a.m. the next day, when she showed up at her parents and introduced Jeff and told them they were in love. She said she was going to divorce me, and they were going to get married.

On February 27, two days after my birthday, she and Jeff moved the kids into Roy and Gladys's house. Her parents didn't agree with this, and they videotaped them putting the crib together for video evidence. By March 5, she moved back in with me after the counseling of friends from church and a warning by the preacher that she and Jeff should discontinue the affair immediately.

I was so lonely and confused that I began searching for love in the wrong places. Susan and I rarely had sex anymore, and when we did try, it was meaningless for both of us. I had opportunities to possibly pursue affairs, but I had a wife and wanted our marriage to work, so I resisted the temptation. I didn't want a relationship with anyone else.

One night, I found myself in a park, trying to just see clearly the mess my life had become. I needed time alone to think. There was a knock on my window. I looked up to see a man standing there, smiling. I rolled my window down. "Yes, how can I help you?"

"What're you doing tonight?" he asked.

"Just wasting a little time, I guess, before I go home."

He saw the ring on my hand. "You married, huh?"

"Yes, I am."

"You ever mess around?" he grinned.

"No," I said nervously. That was what Johnny had asked me.

"No, because you don't want to, or no, because you never have."

"Just no."

"Can I get in?"

I thought about it for a minute as I remembered what was waiting at home. I unlocked the door, and he got in.

"You're not a cop, are you?" he asked once he got in.

"No."

I learned that this was how things worked sometimes. If you were patient, sometimes it worked out. Just like when I was eleven, after it was over, I felt like I was going to puke and wanted nothing more than a hot shower, but as things got worse at home, the loneliness outweighed the guilt. I prayed for guidance but heard only silence. There was not any love or true connection with any of the men, but it was release, and for a moment, I could imagine that someone cared about me, wanted me, if only for a few minutes. That was better than nothing. It didn't really dawn on me that this probably led back to what happened with Johnny. I shared a part of my guilt to Susan, who seemed to care less what I was doing.

At home, all I could do was focus on the kids and work. One wintry day, Susan had gone to work her shift and called to tell me that since the roads were getting bad, she'd stay and work my shift, and they would put her up in a room at the hotel next door so she could also work her shift the next day, and that would limit driving on the roads. I agreed to stay with the kids and take care of them. It would only be after the divorce, when I was working once again with our coworkers, that they would tell me she had slept with one of the cooks and had been having a little bit of a thing with him, but they felt helpless to tell me at the time.

The affair continued secretly, and on one occasion while I stayed home with the girls, who were sick, she went to see Jeff and left Adam alone in the car. He woke up and entered the house and would later tell me that his mommy and Jeff were in the bed with their clothes off. He told this to me and his grandparents. We were all in shock that she had no discretion and would leave her son alone in a car! She denied it happened like that, but I didn't believe her at this point.

A little time later, the preacher was doing his sermon, and we were sitting together, holding hands. He said that he had gone by to see a college student who had been involved with someone and found a note with some chocolate chip cookies from the woman who was told to end it. She had baked me and the kids chocolate chip cookies that day. My grip tightened on her hand, and I looked at her quietly, asking if this was she.

That night, we went to counsel with the pastor, and as he questioned her, she threw out that I was having gay sex. That changed the entire temperature in the room, and it became about me. I agreed I had made mistakes but explained that due to the lack of intimacy, I, too, wanted to feel something, and that was the only way I knew. I continued that I was not romantically involved with anyone and was not threatening to leave with anyone, particularly not anyone in the church. I wanted help at least and was willing to take it, but I asked if she was willing to get help and stop her affair. The way the preacher spoke and looked at me, I knew he felt my sin was greater.

On another night, we had gotten ready for church, and I loaded the kids in the car. I sat with the car running, waiting on her to come out. She did come out with a suitcase and said she was leaving with Jeff. She explained she loved him, and he loved her, and it wasn't just an affair. I was shell shocked and got back in the car, not knowing what to do. Adam was screaming, "Mommy!" and the girls were crying as she walked away.

I thought back to my mother leaving my dad, although Adam was a little older than I was at the time. I wondered if I was cursed to relive the crazy cycle that had been my life before.

I moved in with her parents for a brief time, and they helped me get into a house around the corner from them. Several months went by, and things seemed to even out a little. The kids were growing, and I almost felt happy most of the time. Susan still came by once in a while to see the kids. One night, she stopped by after the kids had gone to bed. She told me the affair was over, and she wanted to come home. I was reluctant at first but finally agreed. I told her we would have to find another place to live because her parents would never allow us to live here together because of what she'd done. That's what we did.

Things might have been better for a little while, but they soon came full circle, and we fought all the time. I think that Jeff had been sent home finally, or she would never have come home. Our fights were always loud, and there were names thrown back and forth, and the fights occasionally turned violent.

I realized I had returned to my childhood, but I was the monster now. I was filled with so much anger and distrust that I honestly had no idea how to deal with my emotions. They were out of control. I wanted to fix this but was unsure how. Her solution was that we stay together for the kids and just do our own things. I knew what we had wasn't right, but that wasn't right either, not when we had three children to care for. Something had to change, but I wasn't sure how to go about it. I no longer felt like I had a church or pastor I could trust for support. She convinced me we needed distance from her parents, and we moved into a large Victorian house in Marshall, Texas, sometime in 1991. Things continued much the same with moments of peace, and then we'd start fighting again.

I'd fought depression most of my life, although I wasn't entirely sure it had a name. Now it was swallowing me whole. I was losing control. I just wanted it all to stop. I thought back to when I sat with a knife to my chest, praying for the strength to end my life. I no longer felt it was an unforgiveable sin, but I couldn't imagine leaving my kids behind. Each day became like walking in thick black tar. I pushed until I couldn't breathe.

In February 1992, I was listening to K-Love radio, and part of the programming was about the Minirth-Meier Clinic, and they described inpatient care. I knew things had to change and felt compelled to call the number they'd given. I called from a pay phone at work and spoke with someone. They asked several questions, and one was if I ever thought of hurting myself. The answer was yes. Within twenty-four hours, we had developed a plan for me to go to inpatient care. I made the necessary arrangements with work and at home.

"I think this might be the best thing for you," Susan said. "You've had a tough life, so maybe this will really benefit you, and it might even help us."

In February of 1992, I was admitted into the inpatient facility in McKinney, Texas. The place was comfortable and gave me a slight feeling of security. The staff was friendly, my fellow patients were encouraging as we all tried to cope together, and I didn't feel like I was in a daily battle. I was placed on medications to help ease the turmoil and depression I was feeling. One of the medications was Klonopin, which was to help with anxiety. This is one medication they warned me to ensure I didn't take too much of because it could be lethal.

It was a safe place where I finally felt at rest. The tensions were still there, but I felt like I was surrounded by people who really did care for the first time in my life. One evening, one of the workers rented us the movie *Planes, Trains and Automobiles*. It was such a needed breath of fresh air, and I laughed harder than I ever had in my life. I felt like I was maybe turning the corner for the first time.

We had group therapy as well as some one-on-one counseling with one of the doctors. "Do you prefer Robert or Bobby?" the doctor asked on our initial visit.

"I don't know," I replied. "I go mostly by Robert now, and Bobby kind of reminds me of my childhood."

"Why do you think you are here?" he asked.

I tried to gather my thoughts. "I think my immediate desire is to save my marriage and learn how to be a better father to my kids," I began. "I grew up in a childhood filled with physical, mental, verbal, and sexual abuse, and I know that affected who I am today and how I deal with things, but it's really torn my marriage apart, and I just don't like who I've become. For many years, I've been deeply depressed, angry, and frustrated because I had no idea how to break free of all the pain in my life."

The doctor nodded. "Any one of the abuses you mentioned would be enough to cause problems into adulthood, but with all of those considered, I'm sure you've had a tough time of it. Have you sought counseling before now?"

"Yes, I've done a little counseling here and there, but I never felt like I could be totally honest or open to really delve into my issues. There was a part of me that was trying to protect myself from looking like a bad father or husband, and I had tried to bury so much of the abuse that I really had no idea where to begin."

"That's what we are going to do here," the doctor reassured me. "This is a safe place, and I want you to be completely honest and open no matter how hard it may be. I want you to trust me and know I only want the best for you. I will be by daily to speak to you, and we can find a solution together. How's that sound?"

"That gives me hope, and hope is one thing I've needed for a long time," I shared.

We talked for a little while longer, and he explained the different therapies I'd be involved with and how things worked. Once he was gone, I sat on my bed and cried. They weren't just tears of unhappiness but ones of hope for a better future.

"Robert, let's talk about your childhood. What do you remember most?"

"Mostly, I remember it was bad."

"How do you mean *bad*?"

"There was verbal, physical, and mental abuse…and"—I paused—"sexual abuse. I was surrounded by it, and I felt alone in my suffering."

The doctor wrote on a tablet. "Let's talk about the abuse. Start wherever you want."

I talked for a long time, and he listened patiently, scribbling as I spoke.

"Okay, let's focus on your medication, getting plenty of rest, and know that I'm here if you need me. We're all here to help you feel better."

I made a few friends, and one of the patients gave me a book, *Free to Forgive*, which had helped them. It was a daily inspirational book. Each morning began the same, with us rising and getting ready, and I read a chapter out of the book I had been given. We'd have breakfast, and at some point in the morning, one of the counselors would come by to visit with me.

I did the best I could to open up about the details of my childhood and weave in my marriage and the problems we were encountering. It was hard, but it felt good to finally talk about the things that were difficult to share. One afternoon as we talked about the sexual abuse, I broke down. "I feel so guilty," I sobbed.

"How old were you when it started?" the doctor asked.

"I was around eleven, I think."

"You were a child and were asked to make an adult decision. There's no way you should have even been asked to do that. Let me give you a scenario, and I want you to just be honest with me."

"Okay."

"I want you to imagine that you are sitting in a chair in a room all by yourself. The room is pitch-black. There's no windows or light of any sort. Someone enters the room, but you don't know if they are male or female. You can't see anything. Someone begins touching you. Their hand touches your crotch and begins rubbing. How do you think you would respond?"

"I'm not sure, but I guess my body would respond to the touch."

"So, you'd get hard?"

"Yes, I suppose I would."

"And if they performed an oral act on you, do you agree that your body would respond in such a way that would end in orgasm?"

"Yes, I think so."

"So," the doctor concluded, "it wouldn't matter if the person was male or female, if you knew them or not. Your body would respond to the physical interaction. Then take into consideration that you are still a child and one who is at the beginning of your puberty with hormones running wild. Your life is filled with people you can't trust. You're dealing with so much abuse. You responded the way anyone would have.

"Now think about all the other stuff you were dealing with. Most predators prey on innocents, and somehow, they seem to be drawn to the most vulnerable. They use that to their benefit. You had so many other things on your plate that one more violation of your rights was inexcusable. And then consider this is someone who is an adult in your life who you've come to trust. Spoken or unspoken, we are taught from an early age to respect and listen to our elders."

I had never thought of it in this way, and it gave me a slight edge of peace. I felt like a small weight had been lifted from my shoulders.

We also had group therapy, and I found it easy to see solutions for when others would talk of their problems but didn't realize I wasn't fully applying the same wisdom to my own life. I'd share advice that seemed reasonable and appropriate, but using the same thought process on my pain was difficult.

One of the art projects we did was to imagine our inner child and how they played a part in our lives today and to draw that. After some thought, I drew a child kneeling on one side of a wall with a man standing on the other side. The child I named Bobby, and the man was Robert. The counselor asked me what it meant, and I explained that I had built a wall to protect Bobby from all that he had experienced. They asked me to label the bricks. Fear, anger, pain, confusion, broken trust—one by one, I tried to list all the things I was protecting my inner child from. They told me what I needed to do was to try to take each brick one at a time and pull it out of the wall until the wall was down so that I could embrace my inner child and find healing instead of just building a wall to protect him because he was alone and afraid. That made a lot of sense, and I tried to do just that within my counseling.

One morning, the doctor came by and asked how I was feeling. "Better, I think," I told him with a slight smile. "Things seem to be starting to come together for me, although I know I have a long road ahead, but I at least am beginning to see some hope."

"Very good," the doctor agreed. "Today, let's talk more about the physical abuse from your stepmother."

"Okay," I nodded, looking down.

"I know it can be painful revisiting old wounds, but I want you to feel safe and know that it can help just talking about the things that happened. How old do you think you were the first time Marcella spanked you?"

"I don't know, maybe five or six, but I'm not sure exactly."

"Tell me about what you remember from the first time."

"Well," I said, "I think the first time wasn't so bad. I mean, it wasn't like some of the other times as I got older. She made me go to my room and wait for her, and then I think she spanked me with her hand."

"Did she tell you why she was spanking you?"

"I think so. I'm not sure even what I'd done, but it had made her mad for sure. I don't remember her looking so angry before."

"How did you feel?"

"I was scared, shaking a little. I was sad that I had made her mad. I felt sorry for whatever I'd done to upset her."

"Did the spanking hurt?"

"A little, but I guess it wasn't terrible, not like other times… later."

"Tell me about some of the other times."

I shivered, as if the temperature in the room had dropped. "There was the first time that she started using the belt, my belt. She made me go get it for her."

"Why do you think she used your belt?" he asked.

"I think she felt like her hand wasn't enough."

"Enough? What do you mean?"

"Like it didn't hurt enough. It wasn't working."

"Working? Why do you say that? What was supposed to be working?"

"Making me stop being bad, doing things that were wrong."

"What were some of the reasons you remember being spanked for?"

"Talking back, not picking up my things, not doing the dusting right or missing something when I vacuumed, dropping a dish on the floor, getting in trouble at school, not doing something fast enough or getting something done that I was supposed to have done."

"Okay," he nodded. "What did she say to you before she spanked you for doing these things?"

"She said that I'd been bad, that I screwed up. I couldn't do anything right." I paused. "She'd say I was stupid. Sometimes she called me a fucking idiot, nasty little son of a bitch."

"That sounds like those things she said bothered you?"

"They hurt. They made me feel ashamed. I felt bad, like I was bad, or something was wrong with me."

"Do you think you were bad?"

"She said I was—"

He stopped me. "Not what she said. I want to know what you thought. Did you think the things you did were reason to be spanked?"

"Maybe sometimes. I don't really think some of the things deserved a spanking, but I guess she wasn't happy about the things I'd done."

"How many times would she spank you with the belt? How many times did she hit you?"

"Ten or twelve times maybe. Sometimes I couldn't even count them because it felt like it went on forever. I'd fall to the floor, crying sometimes, hoping she'd stop."

"And did she?"

"No. Sometimes she just kept hitting me on the floor, and other times, she'd jerk me up and tell me to stand still, or she'd give me something to cry about."

"How did that make you feel?"

"I was scared, terrified even. I always thought that saying, 'I'll give you something to cry about,' was stupid because wasn't what she had already done enough to make me cry? I was afraid of her. I could always tell when I'd done something wrong because she got this look in her eyes, and it frightened me. I knew what was coming."

"Do you think there's a difference between a spanking and what some would call a beating?" the doctor asked.

"I guess I never really thought about it, but yes, I think there is. What I got in the beginning was maybe a spanking, and what came later was what I would call a beating. I felt beaten. I used to pray that God would help me not be bad anymore so they would stop."

"Do you think you were bad?"

"I think I felt like I must have been, or why would she do those things to me? She made me feel like I was bad."

He smiled at me softly. "Part of being a child and growing up is learning to make decisions on your own. Sometimes you may make the wrong decision or do something that was what she called bad, but no matter what you did or what you chose, those choices don't mean you are a bad person. It just means that sometimes *you* made mistakes. Would you agree with that?"

"I guess now it makes sense. I really don't think dropping something or missing a piece of dust meant that I was stupid or really bad," I agreed.

"Do you think that dropping a dish deserved a spanking, a beating?"

"No." A tear slid down my face. "I don't think anything I did as a child deserved what she did to me. She made me undress before she hit me, sometimes down to my underwear and sometimes even more so that I was naked."

"Why do you think she did this?" he asked quietly.

"Because...it made her feel powerful and made me more vulnerable. The belt hurt more on bare skin than going through clothes."

"So it sounds like you are saying she wanted to hurt you even more than perhaps she had done before."

"Yes. I think she liked it, hurting me. She had this evil grin, and I'd see it as she'd finish or when she'd tell me to go to my room."

"Did you ever tell your dad what happened?"

"I was scared to for a long time because she'd tell me if I told my dad or my brother, that she'd make me sorry that I did, and I really believed she would. One time, he did see some of the bruises and welts she left, and he asked me who did it to me, and I told him it was her."

"What did he do?"

"He seemed really angry and said that she'd never do that to me again. But she did, a lot more. That's when I knew I was alone. No one was going to help me. There was nothing I could do."

"That's a scary thought, especially for a young kid—to think you are alone and unprotected."

I nodded. "It was. I prayed when it was over, and I was laying in the floor, crying. I'd pray that God would stop her, that He'd send someone to save me. But then it would happen again, and I think I felt like even God didn't love me."

"Do you think that's true, that God doesn't love you?"

I hesitated. "I believe today that God loves me and that He loved me then. I know now that I wasn't alone in what happened. It happens to a lot of kids. I didn't understand it then. I don't even think I understand it completely now why God allows things like that to happen. There's so much bad in the world that doesn't make sense. Serial killers, rapists, child molesters, and people who abuse children—why would God want that in the world?"

"What is the answer? Why does God allow so many bad things to happen," he asked me.

"Good people die, and bad things happen to good people. I don't think God wants those things to happen, but He gives us all choices, and some of us make very bad choices. I think if all the horrible things weren't in the world, that we'd be in heaven, and this is the world, not heaven, so a day will come when it will all go away, but for now, we have to live with it. I think it must make God very sad when He sees the things that we do in I world, the things we do to each other. I think He is probably even angry at us sometimes at the things we do."

The doctor looked up from his writing. "That seems like wisdom. I'm sure it's hard saying those things out loud, but I think you've learned a lot from living through what you did."

We talked for a little while longer, and then the session ended. I returned to my room, where I looked around, feeling lost and alone again. I lay on the bed, pressed my face into the pillow, and let the pain pour out as my body was wracked with sobs, and salty tears flowed down my cheeks. I wept for hours. Grieving the broken child who had become a shattered man. Darkness wrapped its arms around me as I slid into sleep.

"How did you rest last night?" the doctor asked.

"It was a rough night," I admitted.

"That is understandable," he nodded. "The thing about the wounds that the abuse causes is that even when they are completely healed, there will always be a scar to represent the damage. Until it heals, there is a scab, and therapy is kind of picking at that scab and causing it to become fresh and bleed. Over time and by opening up about what happened, the scab will become smaller and eventually heal, but until then, it can cause irritation and pain. It will get better, Robert."

I smiled gently. "That actually makes sense."

"Let's begin. Is there anything specific you would like to talk about today?"

I paused, thinking. "I guess what was hardest about last night was flashes of memories of the things that happened. I could tell you some of those things."

"That's a great place to start. When you are ready, tell me about them. Take it at your own pace, and don't allow them to overwhelm you. You are in a safe place here. Nothing can happen to you."

"One of the things is that I used to wet the bed a lot," I hesitated.

"It's okay," he encouraged. "That is very common with abuse. The stress and anxiety from all the things you were trying to deal with can lead to bed-wetting. There's nothing to be ashamed of. It is simply your body trying to deal with all the stress you are feeling. Do you remember how old you were when it began?"

"Not really. I was young but old enough to do the laundry. But we had to learn to do chores pretty young, so I might have been around eight or nine. She saw me putting the sheets in the washer and asked me what I was doing. I was afraid of how she'd react, so I tried to lie, but she grabbed them from me and could smell the pee. She slapped me and started yelling at me, calling me names—pissant, lazy son of a bitch. It was early, but I could already smell the beer on her breath. I was crying and shaking.

"After that, it didn't happen every night. I would just make my bed over the wet sheets and hope she didn't find out. I'd go to bed and have to smell it and wake up smelling it.

"She eventually caught on. One morning, she came in my room as I was making the bed and shoved me out of the way. She yanked the blankets back and saw the stains. When she turned, her eyes looked almost black. I felt her hands hitting me, and she was cussing and telling me I was useless and no wonder my mother left me.

"I remember her grabbing me, and…and…and she…she shoved my face into the wet sheets and was rubbing my nose in them like some people do with puppies. I had that thought. I felt like nothing more than a dog."

"I'm sure that was very hard for you. No one should be treated in that manner or made to feel that way."

"That's the thing I kept asking myself over the years, 'Who would treat another person like that?' I sometimes believed that she was a demon or something, not human. Or maybe it was me that wasn't human. I just couldn't understand how anyone could have that much hatred and anger for someone else.

"Most nights, when my dad and her were home, we had this kind of ritual and would give them a kiss on the cheek and tell them we loved them before we went to bed. I'm not sure. I guess we always did it. Even when she was doing those things to me, I still said I loved her and gave her a kiss. That's what hurt the most. I *wanted* to love her and for her to love me. She said she loved me, but would she do what she did to me if she loved me?"

"That's a tough one," the doctor admitted. "You told me that your dad and her would fight a lot and scream horrible things at one another. Those fights sometimes became physical. They stayed together all those years, so there was at least something like love to keep them there. To some people, what they had wasn't love, but just because they fought doesn't mean that they didn't love one another.

They just expressed that love in ways that most people wouldn't consider appropriate. She may have loved you but was incapable, for whatever reason, of expressing that love in a proper way. Maybe that's the way love was shown to her when she was young. We may never fully know what it was, but she was dealing with demons of her own."

"I sometimes thought that too," I said softly. "I thought maybe her mom or her dad did some of those things to her, and that's why it didn't seem wrong. To her, it was normal. Now I can see that she wasn't normal. There was something wrong with her. I accepted the blame for it when I was young. I thought I was the problem. I was bad.

"There was this time one night—I'm not sure how old I was—but when I went to kiss her on the cheek, she turned her head and stuck her tongue in my mouth. I pulled back, and she just laughed. She had this evil, cackling laughter that made me afraid. My dad was there, and he just laughed too. I was too young to know about French kissing at the time, but I never forgot that memory.

"She would whisper in my ear sometimes when she was beating me that I should just die or that one day, she would kill me. I believed her. Even the nights I woke up *before* I wet the bed, I would lie there for a minute, listening to the darkness. It wasn't real, I know now, but I was scared she would be out in the hall, waiting for me. Or maybe some kind of other monster would be there to try to kill me, and I was so frightened that instead of going to the bathroom, I would pee under the bed or in the closet. I know that makes me sound like a freak."

"Not at all," he reassured me. "Although as you look back now you see it differently, at the time, through a child's eyes, those monsters were real."

"The den is where we played as kids," I remembered. "It was originally part of the garage, but my dad put up walls and created the room. We spent a lot of time down there. It was kind of an oasis. There was still room for one car in the garage, and that led into the utility room, which was really just a long hallway. You had to pass through the utility room to go into the kitchen, which was part of the house. There was a door that led outside, but most of that hallway was very dark. I was convinced there was something in that darkness. I'm not sure if I was more afraid of what might lurk in the darkness or in the light upstairs where she sat. Even with the light on in the den, I couldn't see all the way down the hallway.

"To go to the bathroom, you had to go through the kitchen and dining room into the living room, and that's where Marcella sat. She was right at the corner of the living room where it connected to the hallway. Sometimes when she was in a particularly bad mood, I didn't want to go past her because it was like poking a bear. You never knew if it was going to attack you, but it was likely that it would, so I'd hold it as long as I could, and when I couldn't hold it any longer, I'd pee in the corner, somewhere out of the way or behind something where it would dry before she'd find it.

"I thought about going outside but was afraid she'd hear the door open, and I'd rather risk her not stopping me and go to the bathroom than answer her questions as to why I was going outside. If she had ever found out what I did, I can't even imagine what she would have done to me. I'm ashamed admitting it now."

"You shouldn't feel shame," the doctor encouraged. "You were shamed then by adults, so you can't allow yourself to become your own enemy. It's sad that a child is so frightened of a person that they can't allow themselves to go to the bathroom. It's the predators who preyed on your fear that should feel ashamed. You were merely protecting yourself from a perceived threat."

I paused for a minute, wiping silent tears on my face, trying to take in what he was saying.

"What other memories do you have of the den?" he asked.

"As we got older, my dad put a TV down there for us, and we had a couch so we could kind of escape for a little while. There was also a refrigerator in the den. Mostly, it was filled with beer. My dad did drink beer, but he was also an Old Charter and Coke guy. The beer drunk was kind of fun. He was kind of quiet, but the more he drank, the more he would be funny, do silly things. As he drank the whiskey, he became mean. That's when Marcella and he would fight, and sometimes it became physical.

"We had to bring her beers sometimes, and he showed us how to mix drinks for him. There were times when he was very drunk and angry and would ask for another drink. We'd add more whiskey than usual each time, hoping that he'd pass out. Mine and my brother's bedroom was right on the corner of the dining room and living room, so when they fought, we didn't sleep much. We were forced to lie there and listen to them screaming insults at one another. There was a lot of cussing, and more times than not, at some point or another, she would bring up 'your f——ing kids' and tell him how useless we were.

"I never got that part. We mopped, dusted, vacuumed, cleaned bathrooms, did the dishes, cooked, mowed the lawn, and worked in the garden, so I couldn't imagine what else she could possibly want us to do to become *useful*.

"There were occasions when the shouting became more violent, and we would hear a crash of him throwing a glass or ashtray at her, or we would hear the shuffling and cussing as they shoved at each other. One night, I remember that they had gone to bed and were still fighting, It was late, and we had school the next morning. Suddenly there was a loud noise, and she was shouting his name.

"My brother, sister, and I went running into their room, and he was standing over her with a gun, pulling the trigger. It wasn't loaded, and the noise was him shoving her out of the bed. I honestly don't know why because you'd think it would be the opposite, but we were always running to her aid and getting between them, trying to stop him from hurting her."

"That's because you were good kids, and you knew what was right and what was wrong. That's what good kids do, not bad ones."

Over the next few weeks, we continued talking about things that had happened in my childhood. Each day became a bit easier, and the pain seemed to fade just a little more. The bad dreams were less as well. "Let's talk about your marriage," the counselor suggested one day.

"We married young, but I truly believe I was in love with my wife," I began.

"I wanted what my brother and sister had—a good marriage, a home, and the kids they'd eventually have. I wanted that white picket fence, two-car garage, happy homelife that I believed was out there. For brief moments, I could lie to myself and believe we had some of that, but reality always seemed to laugh at me from the side. I wanted to be a good husband, but I had no real examples in my life to base that on. I think I just became what I hated most without really wanting to, and the church that we were involved in was my first experience with going to a service on a weekly basis. We didn't grow up with church. Although there were things I knew of, I was being taught so many other things that I had no experience with."

"Tell me about the church itself," the counselor prodded.

"It was a Fundamental Independent Baptist church. I was taught women wear dresses, men wore their hair short, and the King James Bible was what I should be reading. There is nothing wrong with those things. It's just being young and newly married, I believed all those things were what I had to do to be a good Christian. It caused friction in our marriage and confusion in my own walk with God.

"I began to think of God as one of judgment, and if you didn't do what He said, you'd be in trouble. It was replacing the God of mercy and grace that I thought I knew. I felt like I had to be the spiritual leader in the home and hold us both accountable, and if she resisted, our salvation was in jeopardy.

"They preach once saved, always saved, but I didn't want to be backslid or out of God's love. It was hard trying to live up to those standards, but I did learn to pray, and I read my Bible and memorized scripture, although I didn't always understand the words that were written."

"When do you think the trouble started in your relationship?" he asked.

"It was early on," I admitted. "She was young and still in high school, but I didn't like that she hung out alone with guys from school and felt it was opening her up to temptation. I was jealous. I wasn't a good leader but became more of a dictator, although it came from what I thought was right. I wouldn't realize it until much later, but I also think in some way, my relationship with my wife mirrored what I had with my stepmom, and I wasn't going to be pushed down or rebuked any longer. I also wanted her to have everything she wanted, which wasn't realistic in such a young marriage, and this caused financial problems that we fought over and which caused stress in our relationship."

I paused for a moment before continuing. "The first time I knew she cheated on me at some level was after the birth of our son. It was a customer she had at work, and when it came out, I was blindsided. It just fed all of the jealousy and mistrust I had in her, and I never recovered from it. It became harder to believe her, and she made a statement to me at the time that she had never loved me but was only trying to get away from her parents."

"That must have been painful to hear," he said.

"It was," I admitted, "and whether she meant it or not, I could never forget those words, and I'm sure I became resentful of her."

He looked up at me. "Did you have any indiscretions?" he asked.

"No, not at that point. I knew our marriage was far from perfect, but it didn't mean I didn't want it to work. It was only after a few more questions were raised about her faithfulness and the birth or our daughters that I began to have sex with men in parks. It started by accident by being in the wrong place at the wrong time, but I wanted the attention and what I perceived as affection that I wasn't getting at home."

He was looking at me, and I wondered if he was judging me like the preacher had. "Do you think it was possible that once it started, these acts were rooted in what happened to you as a child?" he questioned.

"At the time, I didn't really think about it, but yes, as it continued, I did. It was never about a relationship. It was just a sex act that meant nothing to me, although I know that doesn't make it any less wrong than what she did. There were many things that made me question her faithfulness, but it wasn't until Jeff, a Bible student at church, that I could actually say she was having an affair."

We talked about all that had to do with the affair. He listened patiently, although he had no actual words to make the pain go away.

He told me that he had spoken to Susan and had asked her to come for a session together with me, but she said she couldn't due to the kids or work. Her parents would have watched the kids gladly, and work would have let her off for one day.

At some point, my dad and Marcella came, and we met with them. The counselor asked me to address some of the issues from my childhood, and I did. Marcella just sat with a smirk on her face and denied that anything had happened the way I was describing it. Dad never really denied anything but just listened and, at one point, apologized if there was something he could have done differently. There was no real conclusion or resolution made, but the counselor said it was more important that I was heard at least, and I could control nothing but my own feelings. It was my option to forgive whether they admitted to wrongdoing or not.

My mom and Henry also came, and we talked about how I felt about her leaving us with Dad and how different I think my life could have been had she been able to take us with her. They were apologetic and encouraging, so some healing came from that discussion.

A few weeks later, the doctor said that I'd be going home soon and asked how I was feeling. "Better, I think," I began. "I think I'm beginning to understand things about the abuse, that it wasn't my fault, and I didn't deserve to be treated the way I was. And as for the sexual abuse, I think the most important thing I've learned is that no matter what decision I made or the reasons, I never should have had to make those choices anyway. It's still hard to fully forgive myself for allowing it to happen, but I realize I didn't have anywhere to turn for help."

"Your stay is coming near the end," the doctor said, "and I want to make sure you are feeling confident about what's to come and that you have a plan in place as to how you will take back what you've learned to apply it to your marriage and your life."

"I think I'm ready," I agreed. "I won't lie. It is scary to think of going back home and being unsure of what to expect, but I'm stronger now, and you've helped me start the process of healing."

I returned home to the welcome arms of my children and looked forward to a fresh look at my marriage. We didn't fight for the moment, but I didn't feel any warm embrace from Susan either. She seemed distant, but I assumed it was the time I had been away.

I didn't return to work immediately but transitioned back into my job. I was told that customers, our parents, and several people had provided money to Susan to help her in my absence. But we were still behind on rent. My regulars and coworkers were all very supportive, and that helped.

One day, while I was watching the kids, they told me something disturbing "While you were gone, Mommy was wrestling with a man in the bed," my son told me.

"How did you see this?" I asked.

"We heard voices and thought you were home. We looked under the door and saw Mommy with a man. They were wrestling with their clothes off," he giggled.

I felt the lights go out on my life. Darkness surrounded me like a blanket. I felt like I couldn't catch my breath. All I could do was wait for Susan to come home and figure out a way to address it with her. Could I never win? Had this been what she was doing in our own home while I was trying to find a way to make things better?

"The kids told me they saw you wrestling with a man in bed while I was gone," I shared with my wife. "Is this true? Are you still cheating? Are you cheating in our home with our kids in the next room?"

"How would they see me *wrestling in bed*?" she asked.

"They watched you under the door."

"Well, they should have stayed in bed."

"That's beside the point," I mused. "Are you cheating?"

"I'm not cheating," she said coldly. "Our marriage was over a long time ago. I'm simply moving on with my life, which is what you should do as well."

"What have I been doing these last few months?"

"You should have been working on you!"

"I was, but I thought I was working on us too."

"I wasn't there, and I don't need help. You do."

"You can be such a bitch. I can't believe you'd bring a man into our home, into our bed, with our kids here watching!"

"I finally found a *real man*. I don't care if you understand or not. He's going to get a divorce, and I am too. If you can't understand that we are over, then you really are fucked up!"

"He's married?"

"They aren't happy either."

"Why couldn't you just wait until I got home and we divorced or separated?"

"I've *been* waiting. I'm tired of waiting!"

"I don't want this to go this way!" I pleaded.

"I don't care what you want anymore. I want to be happy! I deserve to be happy!"

"At the cost of your family?!"

"This is no family. You are not my family!"

"I can't live like this anymore," I sobbed.

"Don't. Don't live like this. I don't care what you do, but I don't want to deal with your shit anymore!"

I grabbed the bottle of Klonopin from the counter and poured out a handful.

"Are you going to take an overdose?" Susan asked sarcastically. "If you've got the balls to do it, then go right ahead!"

I looked at the pills in my hand. My kids, my family—what would they think? Would I even be missed. I looked at Susan glaring at me and then swallowed the pills with some water to wash them down.

"You are so stupid!" she shouted. "You won't follow through with that! Go spit them out!"

I turned and walked out of the house and turned the corner into the night. There was a vacant house next door, and I stepped into the shadows of the entryway. I welcomed the darkness that wrapped around me.

I don't remember anything until a flashlight shined in my eyes, and I heard a police officer asking if I was okay. I guess that Susan had called 911. I tried to insist that I'd had a fight and just needed to be alone. He asked if I'd taken anything, and I lied. Darkness swallowed me again.

I woke as they put me in an ambulance and then faded away again. My last thought was that this nightmare was almost over. I prayed that God would be waiting for me at the end of the tunnel.

I stirred. Hands were holding me down, and I could hear voices. I struggled. They were forcing something into my mouth. I begged them to stop. I think I remember throwing up, then I fell into oblivion—no tunnel, no presence, nothingness.

When I finally woke in the hospital, I was alone. It all seemed like a dream, fuzzy around the edges. There was a tube in my nose, and I could see a bag of something black hanging from the IV. I lay there for a minute, and almost immediately, a nurse arrived at my bedside. "How are you feeling, Robert?" she asked with a smile. Her hand patted my arm as she watched me patiently.

"Um…okay," I responded groggily. "A little sleepy."

"That's to be expected."

"Can you take this out?" I pointed to the tube.

"Not just yet. That is helping to absorb the medication we couldn't get out of you by pumping your stomach. Get some rest."

"Please," I begged. "It's so uncomfortable."

"The only way we can take it out is you'd have to drink it. It's certainly not going to taste like a chocolate shake, but it's drinkable."

I agreed and began to drink the charcoal liquid. They removed the tube, and I fell back to sleep.

When I awoke the next time, my father-in-law was sitting by the bed. "How are you doing, son?" he asked.

"Okay, I guess. I'm sorry…"

"Don't apologize," he said. "Just don't try that stupid shit again! You've got kids counting on you."

"I know. I was just…I don't know…done, I guess."

"We've spoken to the hospital you were in, and they can take you back for up to two weeks. Once they release you here, I'll drive you there."

"Thanks for being here for me." A tear crept down my cheek.

It felt like defeat going back into the hospital. No one made me feel like the failure I thought of myself as, and they focused on ensuring I was ready to go back out into the real world. It took a little time, but I came to realize that I couldn't control everything in my life, so I had to do what I could and let go of the rest. I also realized that during my last visit, I was hoping to fix my marriage. This time, I was working to fix myself. I had no control over Susan or the choices she made. I could only help myself.

My first morning back in the hospital, as I read my daily devotional book *Free to Forgive*, I came across a passage, Isaiah 40:29–31.

> He gives power to the weak, and to those who have no might. Even the youths shall faint and be weary, and the young men shall utterly fall, but those who wait on the Lord shall renew their strength. They shall mount up with wings like eagles, they shall run and not grow weary, they shall walk and not faint.

Later that morning, when the doctor came around to check on me, he shared the same verse with me, although in a slightly different version. I decided that would be my life verse. I would find wings to mount up as an eagle anytime troubles arose!

Each day, I grew stronger, and the pain seemed to lighten. I made peace with the fact that I couldn't control Susan's actions or decide for her whether she wanted our marriage to work out or not, and that was a huge leap for me. Once I made that realization, I began to focus on myself and what I could do to make things better for me. I had to become a better man, a stronger man, not only for myself but for the children I loved.

The two weeks passed quickly, and as the day approached for me to leave, I knew I was leaving changed. Susan wanted us to separate, so once I was released, I went to stay for a little while with my aunt and uncle in Dallas.

Eventually, I knew I had to get back to my life and work. I got a small efficiency apartment in town that was above a garage apartment. Susan and I worked together at Denny's, so that was a bit awkward, but we got along better at work than at home, and I was able to know the division of work and our personal life. I was slightly fragile, but I worked hard to build my self-esteem and encourage myself every day. I prayed and read my Bible daily and surrounded myself with encouraging music that played continually—Steven Curtis Chapman; Phillips, Craig and Dean, Steve Green, Sandi Patty, Twila Paris, Ray Boltz, Amy Grant, and other artists. A few good weeks went by.

One evening, I decided to bring flowers to Susan and simply say that I loved her, and if she was able to give me another chance, I was willing to give her one as well. I drove back to the house, and one of the first things I noticed was a red truck by the curb, but I assumed it was for one of the neighbors. I was about to knock when I could see through the blinds that she was in her nightgown but wasn't alone. She was curled up next to a man. My mind raced. I knocked and could see her jump up, and the man left the room.

"What are you doing here?" she asked as she opened the door.

"I just wanted to bring you some flowers. Can I come in?"

"Now's not a good time."

"I could see *that* when I arrived, and you were sitting next to that guy in our home."

"It's not your home," she snapped. "We are separated. I told you I'm done."

"We are now. I hope the kids are in bed this time at least!" I returned to my car and drove away, feeling good that I was able to find the strength to not engage in an argument with Susan.

I refused to give in to the sorrow that was surrounding me and focused on myself and enjoyed what time I had with the kids. Work was a welcome relief from my problems. We ended up losing our house and all of our belongings, except for a handful of things that her parents were able to rescue. Susan quit her job and moved to Louisiana with the kids to stay with her mom.

Around the girls' birthday in May of 1992, Susan and the kids came to stay with me for a few days, and we talked about starting over by becoming friends and learning to date again. I was thrilled by this possibility. I left one afternoon to go to work, and she kept the car. That evening around seven thirty, she dropped the keys off with the car and a note. The note said she needed more time to think and said she was going to Louisiana and stay with her mother.

Later that evening, I got a phone call at work from the babysitter, a friend from church, who told me she was watching the kids, and Susan was supposed to have picked them up by now. As it got later, she was growing concerned. I was surprised that they were at the babysitter since I had assumed they were with her, but I got approval to leave early and went to my car.

I felt cold. I wasn't shocked that much that she was leaving but couldn't understand how she could just walk away from her kids again for what I assumed was the married man she'd been involved with. I went to pick up the kids. The kids were all upset and crying. They said Jackie had followed them to the church, where she left them with the babysitter.

"Mommy was kissing Jackie," my son told me.

The girls wanted to know why she was kissing someone besides their daddy. I had no answers for them. I picked up the phone and called my family. I then called her family. They were supportive and agreed to help watch the kids and do anything they could. I told my landlord what had happened, but after a week, they told me I'd have to move out because it was leased to me and wasn't intended for a man and three children. I reached out to someone at church, and they agreed to let me stay for a week at a house where someone was on vacation.

I had to decide what to do. I didn't totally trust her parents because Susan was their daughter, and though they'd given me no reason to doubt their loyalty, I was afraid they'd try to take the kids away from me, and I couldn't even imagine that.

After discussing with my family, I decided to move back to Oklahoma, where my brother agreed to take the girls, and my mom took my son while I tried to find a job and get us a place to live. We drove to Oklahoma, and with a broken heart, I told my kids goodbye for a little while as I worked to rebuild our lives.

I slept in my car for a few days while I put in applications. I could no longer afford the car payment, so I drove back to Texas to drop it off and then took a bus back to Oklahoma. My dad picked me up at the bus stop and said he wanted me to stay with him at his house until I could afford rent.

"He will *not* live here," Marcella screamed once we got home. "That son of a bitch can figure this out on his own. I'm not going to live in fear!"

Fear? I thought. What had I lived with for almost fourteen years? She was afraid that now that I was grown and could defend myself, I'd attack *her*. The young boy might, but the new man I was becoming would never stoop to her level. I wouldn't become the monster she had been. "Trust me," I told her, "I don't want to live with you either. What happened in the past is over. It's done, but I'll never forget what you did to me." I got up and stormed out.

"Son"—my dad followed—"let me talk to her. We have two rooms sitting empty. We can work this out. Just give me some time."

"I don't want to be anywhere I'm not wanted," I said through tears. "I've been working these last few months with counseling to come to terms with all this." I pointed at the house. "I will not go backward."

My dad paid for a motel room for two weeks. I had already found a job as a server at Harry Bear's restaurant and walked back and forth each day. I enjoyed the time alone to just encourage myself and talk to God.

I tried visiting the girls on their birthday and had a confrontation with my brother, who told me he thought it was best that I not come around for a while. He said that it was too hard on the girls, and they were adjusting fine until I showed up. This placed me in panic mode, where I felt alone again, and I believed my family wanted to separate me from my kids and knew that was never going to happen while I had breath in me. I was even more determined to save my money, find a house, and get them back before they could make any additional steps to distance me from my kids.

I focused on my work and tried to block everything else out. My heart longed to be with the kids again, and I knew the best way to do this was to work hard and save my money. Fortunately, tips were good, and I was made a lead server, so I made more than just minimum wage.

On the last day of my two-week stay in the motel, there was a knock at the door. My dad came in looking tired and sat on the bed. "Son, I need you to pack your bags and come back to the house with me."

"Dad, I'm not going to be somewhere—"

He raised his hand to stop me. "Son, I need you right now. Mom had a stroke this morning and is in the hospital. Please come stay with me for now. We'll figure something out when the time comes for her to come home."

I was shocked. What was the likelihood of this happening *today* of all days? Before I could stop myself, I thought, *Karma's a real bitch, isn't it?*

I moved back home with my dad and took the guest room, my sister's old bedroom. It felt weird at first being back in a place that held so many memories for me. It helped not to be in my old bedroom, which would have likely stirred many nightmares I didn't want resurrected. It was a new time.

After about a month I had enough money that I asked my mom to let Adam stay with me. I found a good day care, and my dad helped me buy a car. Things were going well under the circumstances.

Around June 1992, I received a call from Susan. She said how sorry she was for the way things turned out, and she wanted to try to make things work. I was skeptical, and every fiber of my being was screaming *no!* We talked for an hour or so. In the end, I didn't listen to my own warnings and agreed to meet her at the bus stop in a few days and told her we'd sit and discuss things. I was nervous, scared, but optimistic.

When I saw her, the alarms were all going off in my head, but I tried to quiet them. I let her spend the day with me and Adam. That evening after he'd gone to bed, we sat at my dad's kitchen table and talked. I was wise enough to question, why now?

At one point, I told her I'd never let her come in and destroy what I was building, and if she wasn't through with her affair, we couldn't come to an agreement. She became angry and walked out. She wasn't from here, and she didn't have a car, so I expected her to walk around the block, but when she didn't return soon, I drove around the neighborhood looking for her.

When I returned home, I found her purse in my bedroom and was curious if she had her wallet with her at least. Something told me to look in it, and I did. The first thing I pulled out was a motel receipt with the name of the man she left me for. I looked at the dates, and she had called me from *his* motel room, telling me how sorry she was. I felt sick, betrayed once more. I realized it was one more attempt to manipulate, and maybe she had realized she wanted her kids back.

She showed up within the hour, and I met her at the door, handing her purse. "I found your motel receipt," I told her. "Kept it, in fact, for the divorce, so don't ever call me again. You've had your last chance!"

She left.

I gathered what money I had, found an attorney, and started the proceedings for a divorce. I knew I had run out of chances, and I had long ago given up any kind of sexual acts with my focus now on myself and getting my kids back together.

One afternoon, I had gone shopping with Adam at IG&A and was walking back to the car when I saw a familiar face. My heart began to thud, and I tightened my grip on Adam's hand.

"Hi, Bobby," Johnny smiled.

I rushed past and got into the car, shaking. All the things I wanted to do to him or say to him were swirling through my head, but I knew I had to leave it alone. He had no power over me anymore other than what I gave him, and I was stronger than that. I drove home with tears flooding down my face. My son didn't understand, and he was too young to try to explain anything more than me telling him that that was a bad man.

In the next month or so, I had saved enough money that we were able to find a cute three-bedroom home near my dad that was affordable. Dad helped me furnish it, and I created a home for myself and my kids. The best day of my life was the day I went to get my girls and slept for the first time, peacefully surrounded by my kids. My brother resisted, saying that I needed more time and should just leave the girls with him. I told him I needed my family back together. We were all reunited again, and I found a great day care in town that had spots available for the kids. We began to rebuild our lives, and by January 1993, it was time for the divorce.

I had kept in contact with my in-laws, and on the day of the divorce, they came up to be with me. I'd heard nothing more from my ex-wife, so I had no idea what to expect. What did happen was far from what I would have imagined. She showed up without an attorney but dressed in her Sunday best with a Bible at her side. I had to keep from laughing. My attorney said he would visit with her.

When the attorney came back in the room, he said he needed to speak to me alone. I told him I was fine with my in-laws being present. "Your wife says you are gay," he began cautiously, "and had numerous homosexual affairs. You never mentioned this, so is this true?"

"I don't know if I'm gay, straight, or bi, but the reason I never brought this up is because why does that even matter? I never once had sexual encounters in front of my children, which she did. I never left with a man saying I was in love, choosing them over her or my children, which she did. I'm not currently in any kind of relationship with anyone, much less a man, and I'm not even looking. She can look that part of the perfect Christian woman, but she's far from it. I'm not perfect, but I have built a home for my kids, and they are beginning to become stable."

The attorney turned to my mother- and father-in-law and asked if they knew. "Yes," my father-in-law began. "We knew he struggled with his sexuality, and he told us he'd made mistakes in the marriage, but he's a good man and has always been there for his kids. I've spent a lot of time with him, and though he's not perfect, he's a great father. She left her kids on at least two occasions for a different man each time. I'd trust him with my grandkids, but I would never trust her again."

The attorney smiled. "And you'll say this to the judge?"
"Absolutely," my in-laws agreed.
"Let's do this then."

I won sole custody of the children, and the only visitation she was granted was supervised at her parents. I didn't gloat. I was thankful, though. Now I could continue to move on with our lives and figure out how to put everything back together again. This time, it would work out.

I had been praying and reading my Bible daily, and it seemed to help. I listened to Christian music to help find encouragement. I felt the presence of God in our lives. When I prayed, it felt as if I was laying my head on His lap, and He held me while I talked to Him.

Maybe things were finally going to work out for me. Maybe I could be *normal*, whatever normal was.

Enter Prince Charming

———⋄∘⌒∘⌒∘⋄———

> I hope, by being honest about what happened to me, to help nourish a culture of honesty that might make something different—and better—possible. We really need to squarely face the issue of child abuse in America, and to look at our perversity, our illness.
>
> —Laura Mullen

One thing I learned quickly was that being a single parent was hard, especially if you were a dad. My son was five years old, and my daughters were three. I had a good day care, which certainly helped; a good job where I did very well in tips; and we had a decent and clean home. I don't know how I paid the bills each month, but I did. There wasn't much left over, but I felt the love of my children, and that covered any lack of anything else I felt in my life.

Their birthdays came and went with no word from their mother. It seemed harder at first for my son because he was older, but they all did very well. Occasionally, they'd ask about her, and I'd tell them what I was able to. I didn't disparage her to them because I remembered what that felt like when my dad did that to my mom. I knew they'd make their own decisions as they grew older. We laughed together, cried together, but best of all, we were together, and that's all that mattered to me!

In the summer of 1993, I discovered I had accrued an additional $500 bill at the day care for working additional hours, and I was unable to come up with that amount of money. I wasn't receiving child support either. Roy and Gladys suggested I move back to Texas, and they would allow us to live with them, help me apply for a Pell Grant to go to college, and help with any assistance I might need. They paid the bill, and I moved to Texas with the kids. I applied for food stamps, and though I was initially denied, when Roy went up to the office and demanded to understand why a woman could get support and a man could not, the decision was quickly reversed. I was also approved for the Pell Grant and applied to Kilgore College a few blocks from their house.

At this point in my life, I never thought of my sexuality. I had my hands full with work, school, and raising kids, so the thought of a relationship was the last thing on my mind. I tried to keep in touch with the children's mother as much as I could, believing they needed a mother, not realizing at some point that generosity would later bite me in the butt. If I did it over again, though, I'd do it the same way. I truly believe that had I not stayed in touch, she would have just faded away from them, focusing on her new life. One day, they would all be curious and would reach out, and I didn't want to be the one standing in their way of each other.

She did do a few visits, but more often than not, she would fail to show. One particular day, I told them that their mom would be in to see them later that day. The girls just played with very little thought, but my son sat in his little plastic chair by the street, waiting for her. It broke my heart to watch him sit there waiting, and I tried to coax him away, but he'd always return to wait.

More time went by, and the sun began to set. It became evident that she was not going to show. I had to hold my son as he wept and asked me why Mommy didn't love him anymore. I reassured him that his mommy loved him and just got busy. In reality, there was no excuse. I couldn't help but wonder if that's how I'd felt as a child. Did I cry in my aunt and uncle's arms, asking why my mommy didn't love me? The similarities to my early life made me wonder if I was doomed to suffer the same mistakes as my parents, but I was determined that I would break the curse. The pain would stop here! I would not let the cycle continue!

Sometime in 1993, I went back to Oklahoma to visit, and we went to my dad's house. The girls ran into the kitchen to say hello to Grandma Marcella, and I stayed to talk to their *cowboy* grandpa. They called him this because he was always wearing a cowboy hat and boots. I also went in to speak to Marcella.

After we left, the girls told me that when they went in to see their grandma, she was sitting with her gown up and her legs spread, grinning. They called what they saw as her third eye. I was mortified and decided that although she was in a wheelchair, she was just as dangerous as she had been when I was a kid. I refused to allow this to affect my kids, so I made the decision that I would never go back to visit in the home again until she was gone. I never kept my dad from talking to the kids or prevented them from seeing us, but I made sure it would be in my home under my control if they did visit.

I was able to go to school and get help with tuition as long as I didn't work, which makes no sense at all to me. Roy and Gladys were incredibly supportive and didn't complain. I completed my first two semesters of college and was focusing on what I would major in. I wanted to be a counselor with a focus also on writing, but I also wanted to work in the summer so I had money to spend on the kids rather than just relying on the kindness of my in-laws. They reluctantly agreed so long as it didn't stop me from school. I went back to work at Denny's as a server once again to work through the summer break. It was good being around my previous coworkers, and I loved my job. Work was busy, and I felt like things were really coming together, and then life happened.

I was working late one night and waited on a group of guys who were obviously gay. One of them left their phone number, and I stowed it away. I was flattered at the attention, but did I really want to open that door? Whether I did or not, I finally made the call and spoke with John. We talked for a little while before agreeing to meet for coffee the next day. After getting to know one another, I followed him back to his place. I'd never experienced this part of homosexuality. I knew the dark world but had never attempted any kind of relationship. It felt good and was a little freeing…until my father-in-law heard about it.

He was retired military, so he had very particular opinions about homosexuality. We argued about it, and he told me I was being selfish. I told him I couldn't be alone my whole life. He had someone to love, and I deserved the same opportunity. He called me a faggot, and I stormed out.

My mother-in-law found me shaking with fury and tried to calm me down. "He comes from a different culture and time. Things were different then. You have to give him time to adjust. He just wants what's best for the grandkids."

"What's best," I told her, "is for me to be happy. Just like he agreed in the divorce, it shouldn't matter who I love or who I sleep with. That doesn't change who I am or how I love my children! I am just wanting the opportunity to date, and it's not like I want to marry the guy or anything! I'm working, I help around here, and I'm trying to better myself to go to college. Why can't I date whoever I choose to date?"

"I understand," she said quietly. "Just give him some time."

I later heard them arguing while the kids were away. "If you want those grandkids to be a part of your life," she warned him, "you are going to have to give up your hardheaded opinions and accept that boy for who he is. He loves the grandkids and is a good father. That will have to be enough, or you are going to lose them all!"

I ended up moving out with the kids and moved in with John and Ron, the gentleman who owned the home. We still saw Roy and Gladys, but it was strained. They tried. I tried. It just wasn't the same. Susan and Lee, her new husband, came by to visit on occasion and mentioned how happy the kids were and how much they seemed to like Ron and John. Ron was a fantastic cook and baker, and he taught me a lot in that area. We organized and cleaned up a vacant room and made it into a bedroom for the kids and me. The relationship with John never fully formed into anything else, but we had a great time together and developed a friendship.

It wasn't easy for my father-in-law to accept, but he tried. As the years passed, he surprised me time and again by defending me and supporting the choices of one of his gay nieces. I had to allow myself not to judge him so he wouldn't judge me. I'd look back and realize that I'd never found more support than with him and my mother-in-law.

Ron eventually helped me apply for Section 8 housing, and after a few months, I was approved for a three-bedroom apartment not far away. I got all our items moved in, and we settled into our own home once again. I was still working at Denny's. My relationship with John did not go any further, and I did not seek any other form of relationship, sexual or otherwise, with anyone.

At Denny's, we were training a man named David to become a manager, and we became friends over time. This was in 1995. He kept trying to convince me to apply for another management position in Memphis, Tennessee, which is where he was going. It took me some time to think it over, but I finally decided that I needed something more stable than serving tables. He said we could look for an apartment large enough for all of us until we got our feet on the ground. He had been a single dad as well, and so he understood how challenging that could be.

I was offered the position, and within a few months, we had moved to West Memphis, Tennessee, and moved into a nice town house, where the kids all had their own rooms, and David and I shared a bedroom with twin beds. It was a relationship of circumstance and convenience and never became romantic or sexual. I was doing whatever I could to financially provide for the kids and provide them a clean and decent home we could be proud to live in. The kids continued to do well in school with As and Bs mostly, and they loved the large pool we had in the complex. They also had several school friends in the area they could play with.

I continued to encourage a relationship between the kids and their mom. I believed that was the right thing to do. She saw them occasionally, although it was sporadic, and she rarely even called to talk to the kids.

It was expensive living in Memphis, and neither one of us really enjoyed the Denny's we were working at because of the way it was run. We went to visit his mom and aunts, who were the sweetest Christian ladies ever, and they pampered the kids with their love.

We eventually began talking about getting a place in Alabama, which would be nearer to his family, and we'd both try to get jobs in that area. In October of 1995, we moved to Vernon, Alabama, to a nice trailer out in the country. I ended up getting a job at a restaurant in Columbus, Mississippi, which was a short drive away.

The kids resumed school and continued to do well. We lived here until the end of the school year, and at that time, I moved back to Kilgore, Texas, where Roy and Gladys helped us move into a trailer around the corner from them. I thought being nearer to their mother would inspire more visits from her, but it did not. She never met the kids' teachers or came to any programs she was invited to, and she never initiated any visitation at her parents' house, which is how it was set up in the divorce. I went back to working as a server at Denny's in Longview.

During my time in Texas, David had started selling PrimeStar satellites and was doing very well. He invited me to come and sell them with him and see if we could do even better financially as a team. In 1997, I agreed to move back, and we lived a short time in a duplex in Vernon, Alabama. We shared the double duplex for a while, and I would later move with the kids into Hamilton.

Just before school started back, I found a beautiful home in the country in Vina, Alabama, and the kids and I moved there. David and I were still friends but no longer lived together. I was working for McDonald's as a manager-in-training to hopefully become general manager of the new location they were opening in Vina. We had great landlords, and there was so much room for the kids to play. They would ride the bus home if I was working and go to the landlord's house, which was behind us, or to the landlord's relatives' house across the street.

During the 1997 school year, Susan convinced Adam to come live with her, which I allowed against my better judgment. But because I loved him and wanted him to be happy, I gave him that opportunity. During spring break in 1998, when Adam came home to visit, he was crying and saying he was unhappy and asked to come back to live with me. Since I had custody of him anyway, I chose to let him stay. He joined school with the girls, and for the first time, they were involved in cheer, and he was in football. The only time the girls' grades suffered was when they went down some while Adam was with his mom, but they came back up once he returned to live with us.

In August of 1998, Roy and Gladys came in for my son's twelfth birthday, and I was involved in hiring for the new restaurant. That afternoon, I got a call from their grandparents, saying they had not gotten off of the bus. Panicking, I called the school to inquire and was told that their mother had picked them up. I explained that I was the custodial parent and had supplied them with the information at the beginning of school. They told me they didn't know, but she had paperwork, so they had to comply.

I rushed home, and we called the police. They said they'd send someone out to take a statement. Five hours later, the sheriff arrived to deliver paperwork, stating there had been a change made in custody. My ex-wife had been awarded custody. I felt as if my life was crumbling around me. The three things I had been fighting for, living for, were gone.

I would not discover the real truth as to how she got custody until my dad died, and I found papers that my ex-wife had mailed him, showing that she had come to the court in Oklahoma and told them I was secreting the children from her, there was concern they were at risk for abuse, and their homosexual father was involved in several gay relationships. She also used my dad against me by telling the courts that I had not allowed the children to see their grandparents in five years. She was too self-centered to understand it was because I was protecting them from a predator.

How she was able to do so with no proof, I still don't understand. She used the court's bias against homosexuality to win custody. The truth was that she had no parental rights other than supervision at her parents', although I had gone well above that to ensure she spent time with the kids. How could you secret children from a parent who had your address and phone number and had multiple visitations over the last year? We had even spoken on the phone a few weeks prior, and her husband threatened to come there and shoot me because I refused to allow them to talk to the kids after we were arguing over unpaid child support. I reminded him that his wife never paid child support, and her part in the kids' life had always been only at her convenience.

I had never had any allegations of abuse brought against me by anyone, nor would I ever even consider abusing my kids. I barely spanked them because I didn't want to cross into my childhood territory. Yes, I would classify myself as homosexual at this point because I knew I never wanted another relationship like mine and Susan's, but I had been in one two-month relationship in five years since our divorce. That was it. I didn't have time for relationships because I was focused on raising my children.

Roy and Gladys did hire an attorney, and over two months, I was allowed only a few phone calls with my children, where it was obvious we were being listened to because they were very distant and made only general comments. This began to wear me down, and I felt the tendrils of depression trying to wrap around me like the arms of an octopus, but I shoved them back with as much will as I had.

At one point, I fell on my knees before God and prayed. "I don't know what else You want from me," I wept. "I've tried to be as close to You as I could, and I've put my life into loving these kids and providing for them. I don't think I can go on without them. I won't ever try to take my life again, but if You have mercy, surely You will bring death to take me away from this troubled life!"

He heard but didn't answer in exactly the way I wanted. That is one thing I'm thankful for. We think we want exactly what we pray for, but sometimes we get things exactly the way they should be, though we may not see it that way at the time.

At the same time, one of my fellow manager trainees came over one evening and confided in me that she had been having an affair with our boss at McDonald's, and she felt it was going to possibly have something to do with her being asked to be general manager of the new location, and she couldn't stand living with that knowledge. I was shocked but not entirely angry with her. I actually appreciated her honesty. She told me if I didn't think we could work together that she knew of a job at Belmont Homes, a company that built trailer homes.

I decided under the circumstances that I would interview for that position and ultimately took it. I started out in the return warehouse and decided I'd be the best returns worker I could be. I cleaned and organized the warehouse, and my hard work eventually paid off, and I was offered a new position in the warranty department, where I would pull items and stock for repairs that were to be made to the homes. I once again set out to be the best at that as I could. I was later offered a position in the office processing invoices and doing billing.

Our first court date in Alabama was before what appeared to be an older judge who was extremely prejudiced against the fact that I was gay because once that came out, he wasn't moved by any other evidence. As I entered the courthouse, I saw my children across the street, and though I believe they saw me, they all had their heads hung low and barely looked my way. I was crushed. It was obvious that they had very specific orders on how they were expected to behave because I had always been extremely close to them. I felt in my soul that I was never going to win. I was never going to be able to fight against the bias of my being gay. How I loved my children and cared for them each day or how I always ensured they had a clean home that was safe and free from abuse or drama wouldn't matter to this judge.

After several months with no visitation, I told my attorney that I would agree to the change in custody if I was allowed generous visitation, and once my kids became older, they could make up their own minds. I was tired of not seeing them. I was tired of politics. I just wanted to see my children. We came to an agreement that I could live with for the time being. I believed God would rectify this in time.

I had not been alone for any length of time since my children had been born. I had no idea what to do with myself. I was miserable and lonely. I needed some type of connection, so I began going into AOL chat rooms. I rarely spoke, but I lived vicariously through their words.

One evening, I did get a person to reach out to me, and we began talking. I instantly felt a connection, as if I had reconnected with a best friend. He introduced himself as Tim. We talked about my kids, church, hobbies, books, and movies. He was different than any other guy. He didn't ask for pictures or go straight to talk about sex. I began to look forward to signing on to see if he was on. It took my mind off the loss I felt.

We talked for several weeks before we finally decided to meet. We made arrangements to meet at a steak house in Florence. At the last minute, I freaked out, thinking, *What if this guy is a serial killer or a weirdo?*

I waited until he came back online later that evening and confessed. We had a good laugh and decided to meet the next night. I actually followed through this time. He had given me a brief description of what he'd be wearing so I'd know whom to look for. I sat in the parking lot waiting and saw a man who fit the description enter the restaurant. He was very handsome, but I knew appearances could be deceiving.

I got out of the car and went to meet him. We met in the lobby, and as we sat down to eat, it began to feel like we had known each other longer. I was having dinner with a long-lost pal. We got along great, and though I was typically a quiet guy, I found myself relaxing and talking. I shared my experience about what happened with the kids. He was kind and understanding. We talked for hours, and he invited me back to his house for a movie. We rented the Kevin Kline movie *In & Out*. We also watched Jim Carrey's *Doing Time On Maple Drive*. It was a perfect night. I discovered his favorite movie was *Beaches*, but he did not own it.

We continued to meet back online and talked for hours. We planned another date for the next weekend. I arrived with a bouquet of flowers and a VHS tape of *Beaches*. It was another great night, and I could barely wait until we could meet again. I felt I had found my soulmate but realized it was too soon to get that carried away. I just enjoyed the time we had together. It was a welcome breeze of fresh air from all the stress of court and all that was going on with the kids—maybe even an answer to prayer?

We couldn't get enough of one another, but an hour's distance wasn't always easy to make work with our schedules. If I wasn't able to come to his house, he came to mine, and we spent our nights together as often as we could. A week into the relationship, I told him that I was falling in love with him but didn't want him to tell me until he felt it as well. It took a couple weeks more before he said the words, but I will always remember them. It occurred on our way home from a Halloween party. We'd gone to a friend's house, and on the way home, just after midnight, he turned to me as we drove in his Explorer and told me that he loved me.

Things grew fast from there. We decided that since we spent all of our time traveling back and forth between houses, it made sense to just move in together. So in January of 1999, we did just that, and I relocated to Florence, Alabama. I have never looked back with regret.

My family, including my dad and Marcella, welcomed him with open arms, and my children loved him. The girls were nine years old, and my son was eleven years old, so I didn't introduce him as my boyfriend but as my friend. When they were ready, I'd explain it further. However, Susan felt it was important to notify the kids that Tim and I were in a gay relationship, and they were going to *confront* me with it when we came for a visitation.

There was nothing to confront me about because Susan was already aware of my relationship years earlier with John, which she never showed opposition to, and I had not tried to hide that Tim and I were in a relationship. I just felt when the kids were ready to know more, they would ask on their own.

The kids later told me that they were told that they should be prepared for me to just walk out and not come back. Ultimately, that is what she wanted to do—destroy our relationship—but she had no idea of how strong our relationship really was. It did nothing to drive a wedge between me and the kids.

Every day I spent with Tim was better than the day before. We got along great. Not that everything was always perfect because that doesn't really exist, but with my newfound strength, I was bound and determined not to fall back into arguments when we did disagree. He would say I was patronizing him, but I truly wasn't. I just didn't want to fight. I knew where that led, and I didn't like who I became in the past. I had lost the opportunity to show Susan I could change, so I made this my new goal with Tim.

BROKEN TOYS

After moving to Florence, I quit my job at Belmont Homes and began working at Ruby Tuesday and took extra shifts in the evening at Outback Steakhouse. Eventually, Outback led to an opportunity where I did prep during the day and was a head wait in the evening, where I had a good station during the rush and did paperwork afterward, which fed my desire for management. I accepted that offer and became full-time at Outback.

I did well in tips and really enjoyed the entire experience. In early 2001, one of my regulars offered me a job as manager at a local country club. After a lot of thought, I decided it would be a natural step for me to get to a definite salary rather than the ups and downs that come when you are relying on tips. It was hard leaving Outback, though, but I had to start thinking about what was best for my future.

In April 2001, my brother called to tell me about an opportunity with a company he had worked for since he was seventeen. Sodexo was hiring for a general manager at one of their locations in Oklahoma. Tim and I talked about it, and I couldn't even visualize a life without him, but we felt I needed to at least do an interview and see what it was all about.

I drove to Oklahoma City and did the interview. It went well, but I left without any definite decision made. Within a week or so, I received an offer and had to start the discussion with Tim on whether I should take it. The pay was great, and the benefits were excellent, so we decided I should accept. Of course, I immediately asked him to come with me. He was a teacher and had been a part of education in Alabama for thirteen years. He was also in daily contact with his mother and close to his family, so his initial decision was that he couldn't leave it all behind. I still had some time before I had to report, and school would be out by then, so I just focused on what I could control.

One day, on my way home, I heard a song that I shared with Tim. It was Uncle Kracker's "Follow Me." I joked that it was a sign that he was supposed to follow me to Oklahoma. He was very concerned with the approval of his parents and didn't want to disappoint them. We eventually went to a counselor who helped us talk through the pros and cons of both options. One day, he asked a simple question of Tim. "You are very keyed in to the approval of your parents and think if you tell them you are moving, they will be upset, so I have a question for you," he started. "Think of a time when you had something that was important, and you had to share it with your parents. How did that turn out?"

Tim thought for what seemed like minutes and then answered, "It wasn't as bad as I thought it would be."

"So," the counselor continued, "this is your decision to make and though they might not like it, it will likely not be as bad as you think it will be."

This helped to guide Tim into the decision to follow me to Oklahoma. He began to search online for teaching jobs, and though he did not have a definite position yet, he did the difficult part by telling his parents. Though they didn't understand or want him to go, they still supported him as much as they could with the decision he made. It didn't turn out as bad as he imagined, but when he came home, he had a panic attack, and I had to talk him through it.

After school was out, we moved to Oklahoma in June. The day we were moving, I had left the U-Haul running with our cocker spaniel Cassanova in it. I was standing on the porch and noticed the truck slowly rolling forward. Apparently, Cass had hit the gearshift. I began to run to catch up with it and was able to jump in and put in park before it hit anything. I told Cassanova I appreciated he was in a hurry to move, but he needed to be patient.

Tim would get a position at the end of July. We lived with my brother for about a month before finding a house that had been split into apartments. We had the bottom apartment, which was the largest, and we began the process of moving in. Our first night there, Tim's car got broken into, and they stole some CDs. What was amazing is that his wallet was over the visor, but they didn't take it. Within a month we had our bikes stolen from the front porch. We began to question the safety of the neighborhood.

We lived there for about eight months when one night, Cassanova was barking in the dining room in the middle of the night. I got up and tried scolding him to stop. As I entered the dining room,

I saw what he was barking at. We had a door that went out to the porch, and that is the one we used to enter and exit the building. The other door, which was the main door, we did not use, so we had a large bookshelf set against it. That door was open a couple of inches. We decided we didn't feel safe there anymore and began to search for somewhere else. We found a home in Edmond and moved there in April of 2002.

    I didn't really ask the children if they were happy with their mom and stepdad or what went on in their home because I didn't want to cause any trouble or interfere with their lives. I believed when the time was right and if they wanted to live with me, they'd bring it up. That time came in 2002. The kids began telling me that they were spanked with a boat oar that had holes drilled in it, and they were scared of their mom and stepdad. The girls told me of a time when their mother was trying to show them how to use a tampon. They said she demonstrated on herself, and when they were still scared, she told them to use baby oil *so it would slide right in*. When the girls were hesitant to try, she told them, "If you can't handle putting a tampon in yourself, what makes you think you can handle a man's penis going in you?"

    It was like a dam breaking. Once they got started, they didn't stop for some time telling me things that were said and things that were done. One of the more horrifying things was that Susan told the kids in graphic detail what she imagined we did in the privacy of our home. They asked what she meant, and I told them it wasn't age appropriate to discuss, but what people do in the privacy of their homes is their business and was not something their mom should have talked to them about, especially because she had no idea *what* we did.

    At this point, I decided I could no longer sit by and pretend they were happy and being raised in a healthy home. I hired an attorney, and we brought the kids to a counselor. Susan was furious when she found out and threatened to take away *all* of my rights because her children deserved much more than a faggot for a father. I assured her that I was much more than a *faggot* and that a person's sexuality had no bearing on what kind of parent they could or could not be. I also told her it seemed odd that she felt that way since she had left her children more than twice for another man she loved and then married a completely different man. She had not utilized her supervised visitation with her parents, with a few exceptions, and I had gone out of my way and gone against the court's orders and my better judgment to allow her to see the kids beyond what she had been given by the judge. A good parent is one who sticks by the sides of their children during good and bad times, and that's what I had done!

The custody battle was an excruciating nine months, and I picked up a second job in the evening at Outback as a server to save money for an attorney. The children were not allowed to talk to me or their grandparents in the courthouse, so we learned to speak through smiles and gestures. I did win custody of the girls, and my son chose to stay with his mother for reasons I never fully understood but didn't question. The best part of the whole thing was when the judge made his order, he told her that he had no idea how she ever got custody because had it been his courtroom, she never would have been given custody. Again, I didn't gloat but was just thankful for it to be over.

She immediately informed me that we were to pick up all of their things, and anything left would be thrown away. We rented a U-Haul and did just that. I had at least a part of my family back together. Neither of us had to pay child support, although I had two, and she had one, but I didn't care about the money. She was ordered to pay her back child support, which she never did.

Working on the Fairy-Tale Ending

Child abuse casts a shadow the length of a lifetime.

—Herbert Ward

We lived in a nice three-bedroom brick home in Edmond, and it was great to have the walls filled with the laughter and joy of my children once again. It was not always joyful, but I loved having at least a part of my life back together. We lived under a microscope with Susan always watching to see if she could catch one of the girls making mistakes. I tried to explain that's part of growing up, and we both made wrong choices at times, but she was waiting on something big to reverse the custody, and that never happened. Not that they didn't make bad choices from time to time, but I loved them through it and fought for their rights to make mistakes.

Not that I really believed the house was haunted, but we did have some very strange occurrences that we couldn't easily explain away. One evening, Tim and I were watching television, and out of the corner of my eye, I saw movement in the hallway. I looked and saw one of the girls coming out of the bathroom. I went back to watching the show and then suddenly realized they weren't home.

Another time, we brought groceries in and sat them on the counter. They were not on the edge of the sink or anything, but when we went to the bathroom, we heard a loud commotion, and when we came into the kitchen, the bags had been knocked over, and cans were in the sink and all over the floor.

Cassanova was always barking or growling at the corner, but one evening while I was home by myself, I was enjoying a book in bed, and Cass suddenly jumped down and started growling. I looked up, and he was inching toward the bedroom door with his hackles raised and a low grumbling coming from his throat. I knew Tim was in Alabama, and both girls were spending the night with friends, and I remembered locking the doors, so I believed there was nothing to be concerned with. I tried scolding him and calling him back to the bedroom without success. He finally stepped outside the doorway and looked down the hallway and started freaking out. I was too scared to look down the hallway, so I pulled him back into the bedroom, closed and locked the door, and put a chair under the handle. I stayed locked away for the night. We never felt like we were in immediate danger, but we were never able to explain anything away.

We had fun and laughed a lot, but sometimes our humor was slightly different. There was one time that I was dropping the girls off at one of their friends' home, which was very nice, and Catherine stated that we lived in the ghetto. I went home and pulled her television, stereo, and stripped her room down to the bare necessities. When she got home, I took her cell phone and told her *that* was the ghetto! She lived like that for a week but got the point. We might not live in a mansion, but what we had was nice and clean, and that was enough.

On one occasion, I was at a meeting in Dallas, Texas, and on one of our breaks, I noticed I had a missed call from the girls. I checked my voicemail and felt like I was going to pass out from panic. "Dad," Catherine said, "we were coming home from school and crossing the street, and Courtney got hit by a car!"

My mind was racing. I was trying to figure out how to get out of the meeting and back home. I nervously dialed Catherine's phone, and when she answered, I immediately asked if Courtney was okay. She laughed. "Oh, Dad, that was a joke. We were just kidding!"

"A joke," I said sternly, "is when you say what you said, but before you hang up, you say, 'Just kidding,' rather than leaving me to freak out!"

We would laugh about it later, but in the moment, it wasn't very funny although I was greatly relieved that no harm came to one of the girls, especially with me being out of town.

Things are never easy, especially when dealing with teenage girls, but I cherished every moment that we shared. I was also able to enjoy my son on school breaks and during the summer. He was a joy to be around because he always had a way of making us laugh. He was a really good kid and did well in school, as did the girls. We survived the tumultuous teenage years together, and they built long-term friendships that have lasted into the present.

In 2004, we decided to start looking for a house to buy rather than continue to rent and ultimately found a house in Yukon, just six blocks away from where I grew up. I never thought I'd live in Yukon again, especially not that close to all the memories of my childhood, but the price was right, and it had everything we were looking for at the time. It was a rainy day when we moved, and the yard was so muddy, the truck almost got stuck. Fortunately, we had the help of some of their friends to unload everything. We settled into our new home and began to fill it with memories.

One day on my way home, the girls called, saying there was someone in the house. I asked why they thought this. "Dad," Courtney said with fear, "our VCR keeps moving."

"What do you mean the VCR is moving?" I asked.

"It slid across the dresser, and we moved it back, and then it slid again."

I smiled. "Stop playing games with me."

"Seriously," the girls pleaded for me to believe them. "It moved, and when we moved it back, it slid again. We've tried it several times, and it keeps moving."

"Well, if you really think someone is in the house, get out!" I told them. "I'm almost home, and we'll see what you are talking about."

I arrived shortly after, and the girls were waiting in the front yard. Still thinking they were trying to pull one over on me, I laughingly told them to show me the VCR mystery. We went inside to the bedroom, and I moved the VCR. Before long, it slid across the dresser. I turned to them and asked if this was a joke.

"No, Dad, it's for real."

I went into my bedroom and looked in the closet, which was the wall opposite of their room. I expected to see one of their friends hiding in the closet and pulling on the cord, but no one was there. I went back into the bedroom and moved the VCR again. It slid again.

After a couple times of watching the VCR move apparently of its own accord, I told them to get out of the house, and with heart pounding and mind racing, I followed them to the front yard. I wasn't sure how I was going to explain this on a 911 call but was thinking of a way to put it.

Before I made the call, I went around the corner of the house and looked toward the wall of the bedroom. Dangling from the wall was the cord, and our dog had it in its mouth. Every time we pulled the VCR back, the dog thought it was a game and grabbed the cord to pull on it. We had a big laugh, and I was glad I hadn't called 911 yet.

In 2005, we had an event that would ensure I would remember it for years to come. The girls had gone to different friends' houses to spend the night, or so I thought. That evening, I received a call from the police, telling me that they had received a 911 call and arrived at an apartment complex in Edmond to find Catherine lying by the curb with her face in a puddle of rainwater. They had rushed her to the emergency room, and I should get there as soon as possible.

As I rushed to get ready to leave, I called Courtney's phone, but she didn't answer because she was at another friend's house rather than where I dropped her off, and she thought I'd figured it out, and she was going to be in trouble. She drove back to the original friend's home and called me.

"Courtney," I spoke with a wavering voice, "your sister is in the emergency room in Edmond, and you need to get there as soon as possible. There has been an accident or something. I'm on my way there now."

When I arrived at the hospital, I was told by the police that when she came in, she was alert but combative. They weren't sure exactly what had happened but had found her outside, lying in the rain. I was terrified.

Once they got her settled in a room, I was allowed to see her. She was no longer awake and looked pitifully tiny in the bed. "What happened?" I asked the doctor.

"We don't know much at this point, but it's possible she may have been on drugs or drinking. We are currently running tests to find out, and as soon as we know, we'll let you know. She was found with her face in water, so we don't know if there's been any brain damage or not. She was awake when she came in and fighting a lot, but she's now asleep. It's possible she is in a coma."

That sent a chill through my body. Thankfully, Tim was there by my side to give me as much support as he could. He was just as scared as I was. We waited for the test results as I held Catherine's hand in mine and whispered for her to come back to me. Her sister showed up equally alarmed and set about contacting the people Catherine had been with to figure out what happened. It would be some time before we'd get all the details, but she had been at a party she wasn't supposed to be at, and there had been some drinking. She passed out at some point, and after they tried to revive her unsuccessfully, they brought her outside and called 911. We didn't get much more than that.

The doctor came back in the room. "We've run tests for every drug possible, and they were all negative. She had consumed some alcohol, but it was in a very normal range. We are perplexed as to what's going on. As I told you earlier, we are not sure if she will wake up or what she will be like when she does."

I stayed at her side all through the night, praying for her to wake up and everything to be fine. It was a long night, and I didn't sleep at all.

Sometime the next day, Catherine opened her eyes, and I held my breath as we called for the nurse. As the nurse arrived at her bedside, we began asking her questions, and though she was groggy, she was able to answer. *Thank God!* I shouted inside. She would make a full recovery, and we would never know what really happened to bring her to the hospital but were just happy to have her back with us and doing okay.

On Father's Day of 2006, we were all together and having a great day. At one point, Courtney told me she had something she needed to tell me and had written a letter and placed it on my bed. This terrified me, but since the day had been so good, I wasn't expecting anything real major. I went to the bedroom, opened the letter, and began to read. She started off by saying this was the hardest thing she'd ever had to say, but she was pregnant. My legs went out from underneath me, and I fell across the bed. It took me a moment to recover, but I eventually finished the letter.

I did what I could to pull myself together and went back out to find Courtney sitting on the porch. I sat down with her and tried to give her a smile. "This is very difficult for me," I started falteringly, "and I'm not really ready to talk much about it, but I want you to know that I love you, and no matter what happens, we'll get through this together as a family."

"I understand," she said softly. "It just means the world to have your support."

"I'm very disappointed, but there's nothing we can do now but help you prepare for the delivery of this baby and help you be a good mom. It's not going to be easy, but you have my love and full support!"

We did go visit a clinic about adoption, but she ultimately decided she couldn't do that, so we found her a good doctor, and I went with her to every appointment. I could have thrown a fit and screamed and hollered, but it was done, and that would have solved nothing. The focus had to be on having a healthy baby and preparing her for the journey ahead.

She took perfect care of herself and did everything the doctor ordered her to, and in December, Hayden was born. Looking back now, I could not imagine a life without him. He has been such a good kid and a true blessing to us all.

Tim and I decided to go to Ponca City to see the E. W. Marland Mansion in March of 2007. We had a really great time and drove back through Osage County and reveled at the sight of the protected Joseph H. Williams Tallgrass Prairie Reserve, which grew on either side of the road. We stopped in Bartlesville to stay the night and had just gotten checked in. We literally had just laid our suitcases on the bed when my phone rang. It was Adam, and he told me that Catherine had taken our car to see some boy in Lawton and had lost control of the car around Elgin. She was going to be okay but had been taken to the hospital. I called my brother to see if he could go check on her while we traveled back from Bartlesville. We were both livid that she would take Tim's car without permission, but that was eventually replaced by parental concern and relief that she was not seriously injured. The car was totaled, though.

Later in 2007, Catherine told me she was pregnant. It was not ideal, but I was as prepared for it as I could possibly be. I asked that she finish school one way or another. I gave her my love and support just like I did Courtney, and she was also a wonderful mommy-to-be. Courtney was pregnant again and gave me another grandson, Dawson, in March of 2008. In June, Jaxson was born, and I was there to see him delivered. Just like Hayden, Jaxson has turned out to be one of the greatest blessings of my life. Though both girls were young mothers, I think they did as great a job as anyone could have in the same situation.

Courtney gave me and my first granddaughter, Delanie, in September 2011. She had a rough marriage the first time but is in a happy marriage today. Catherine gave me a second granddaughter, Milanni, in March 2012. She also went through a very tumultuous marriage and divorce but is in a healthy and happy relationship today. I told them that they had to stop because they were making me feel like a very old poppy, but I love all of my grandchildren, and they've turned out great!

My dad was diagnosed with cancer in 2008 and had been on dialysis for years. Marcella had been moved to a nursing home because he could no longer take care of her. Fortunately, we had reconciled and grown closer in the years leading up to that diagnosis. He would even apologize for what he allowed to happen to us kids.

In June of that year, my brother and I took off to be with him because he was bedridden and on hospice care. The weekend before, he asked me to take him in his truck to go visit some friends and see the places he farmed. I think he knew time was short. I sat in the living room beside his bed and read a book. At one point I heard him take a deep breath and looked up to see him looking off into the distance. I resumed my book and then heard him sigh, and his eyes were closed again. I was certain he had passed, so we checked to see if he was breathing, and he was not. We called his hospice nurse, and she came over quickly to work with us. I can't say enough how wonderful it was having the support of hospice!

The year 2009 was another life-changing moment for me. February and March were tough months for me. I was feeling very depressed and kept thinking I was hearing voices when no one else was around. It culminated in my making some bad choices in April, which led me to going to see my primary care physician. I had been going to him for years, and he was treating me for depression.

After telling him what was going on, he asked me to take a test. I did, and it showed positive for bipolar disorder, which explained why the depression came and went so much. He changed prescriptions and added testosterone to my therapy. Although it wasn't an immediate change, things turned around quickly, and I began to feel alive again. I lost over fifty pounds easily, which was a great side effect because I was over three hundred pounds at the time and had reached the point where I refused to buy any larger size pants than I was in. This would mark a turning point as well as a reminder for years to come that you had to always stay ahead of the disease. When you feel yourself changing, it's time to go to the doctor and make adjustments as needed.

We decided to make a trip to Branson, Missouri, with my mom and Aunt Eleanor in March 2011. I drove the whole way, and we visited and laughed our way to Branson. We were following the GPS when it told us to turn right onto this dirt road. It seemed odd at the time, but it was supposed to know where we were going, so I decided to follow it.

The farther we drove, the more we realized we were totally lost. It was nothing but rural country, and we eventually came to an overlook. We got out and started talking to a couple who was also there and told them we thought we were lost. They asked where we were going, and when we did, they laughed and said we were off the beaten path, but they would lead us there if we wanted them to. I don't think I'd seen Wrong Turn yet, and we were so desperate to get back on track that we agreed. Fortunately, they were a legitimately kind couple and led us through winding roads until we found ourselves on the outskirts of Branson.

We stayed in a beautiful condo with two master bedrooms. We stayed upstairs, and Mom and Eleanor stayed downstairs. One evening as we were playing Skip-Bo, which was their favorite card game, Tim made a revelation that he thought Eleanor knew. "Isn't it wild how Karen's husband cross-dresses?" Tim said randomly.

Karen was Mom and Eleanor's sister. There was total silence for a minute and then laughter. Aunt Eleanor was blindsided but good natured about it. We all laughed so hard until I thought I was going to pass out from lack of air. Lesson learned—never assume anything! Aside from that, it was a wonderful trip that I would cherish for years to come. I remember eating in the restaurant on the resort and having the best salmon burger of my life. I had never had anything that good before or since.

We took another trip with Mom and Eleanor in October 2015 and went to Colorado Springs. It was another great trip with no unspoken revelations being disclosed by anyone. We made a lot of good memories on that trip. On our way home, we stopped at the Capulin Volcano, and I was the one driving. About halfway up, I began to freak out because there was no railing on the edge, and the road was so narrow that I could not imagine another car coming down. My anxiety was so high, but we made it to the top with no incident. It was not so bad coming down because I had the wall against the car. I will cherish all the memories made on those trips with my mother and aunt.

The year 2017 was possibly the hardest of my life. In May, I was making a career change and would be going out of state for training. I felt close to my mom, but we didn't get as much time together as I wished we had. Though I had a few weeks prior to beginning my new job, I chose to do things around the house and put things in order, giving up time that, upon looking back, I should have spent with my mom. That's the thing about retrospect; you see things differently, but you can never change what choices you made. My son was living with her to help her get things done around the house.

The day I left, I thought about stopping by to say goodbye but decided I didn't have the time. On my trip to the hotel where I'd be staying during my training, I got sick and had to pull over while I threw up in a plastic bag I had in the car. I felt horrible but told myself it was just nerves. I was going to call my mother once I made it in but lay down to rest once I got to the hotel and slept until morning.

My first day of training was full, and I came back tired but had stopped to take pictures of some red yucca plants because they were my mom's favorites, and in Texas, they grew lush and beautiful. I took pictures of my room and sent them with the yucca pictures to my mom's cell phone. I planned on calling her after my shower.

I was drying off when my cell phone rang. It was my son. "Dad, Grandma's gone," he sobbed.

"Gone? Where'd she go?" I asked.

"No, she's gone. She died."

"What?" I felt my knees give out as I struggled to sit down.

"I came home from work, and she was on the porch. She was coughing and trying to catch her breath, but she told me she was fine. She put a pizza in the oven for me and told me to take a shower. When I got out, she was still struggling, and I told her I was going to call someone, but she said she was fine, just having trouble catching her breath. I went to eat the pizza, and when I came out to check with her, she was spitting up some fluid, so I called 911. I laid her down and started CPR, but"—he choked—"she was gone, Dad. I'm so sorry!"

"Son, you did what you could. I will call your aunt and uncle. Are you okay? Do you need anyone?"

"I'm in shock, but I have someone coming over. I'll be okay."

I hung up the phone and crumbled to the floor. I learned a valuable lesson to never wait to call or put off seeing your loved ones because you never know when they will take their last breath. I made the necessary calls, wept inconsolably, and then called my training instructor to notify them that I'd be going back home. I do not know how I made it home safely, but I did. It was raining, almost as if God were crying along with me. I was cold from the shock of losing my mom so suddenly.

It took me several weeks to find the strength to resume my training. Looking back, I saw signs warning what was happening. I believe she died from congestive heart failure. She had undergone a stent placement procedure a few years prior to clear a blockage. She had been experiencing similar symptoms, but when I told her she needed to tell the doctor, she said they would never touch her again because she had been miserable with the first procedure. I tried to reassure her that if she discussed it with her doctor, they might have a solution, and the first stent might have been less painful if she had communicated to the doctor.

She was a stubborn woman, and no one could tell her anything. She was insistent that she didn't want to end up in a nursing home or hospital, so she died just exactly the way she wanted—at home on her own terms.

Her death left a gaping hole in my heart that still aches when I think of her. I would always wonder how different my life might have been if only she had taken me with her the night she fled from my dad. I will always cherish the time that we did have together!

The one good thing that did happen to end out 2017 was that Adam married. His bride, Holly, has been a true blessing to our family, and they have two wonderful girls, Hannah and Bethany. They live happily in Yukon as well.

Tim and I have been together for over twenty-five years, and though we've had some difficult times, he saved me time and again from myself. I cannot imagine a life that doesn't have him in it. He is loved by my children and our grandchildren as much or more as any stepparent. Early in our relationship, I was coming home from work and heard a song that I knew was going to be our song. It was Rascal Flatts's "Bless the Broken Road." It was definitely a broken road for me, but those roads led me to him. It is very much like the movie *Sliding Doors*. If I had not been at Denny's when David worked there, I would never have been given the opportunity to move to Memphis. If I had not moved back to Alabama when I did, I would never have been in the position to even meet Tim. Had Susan not taken the kids from me, I would have not been online looking for human connection, and Tim and I would have never met.

At the time, you may not always know why you are making choices, but I believe God is in control of those moments and can use them to bless you. I know there are people who believe you can't be a Christian if you are gay, but I choose to believe the Bible that says whoever believes in Jesus will be saved. I look at Ray Boltz, who was the number one Christian artist in the '80s. His music touched lives and stirred hearts for God. The fact that he came out as gay doesn't mean his music is any less powerful or touched by God because he was the same person with the same feelings when he made those songs. He only decided to live an honest life for once, and I still weep when I listen to the words of his songs. He has even made some more beautiful music since then.

And Michael Passons of Avalon came out as gay and was rejected by many in the community while being embraced by others. His music is no less significant or blessed because he admitted his true self. God accepts adulterers, liars, thieves, and even murderers. He loves each person as if they were His own, and all He asks for in return is for us to love Him back and accept the sacrifice of His Son. Fortunately, He isn't a God of hate but rather one of love. I spent many years praying to be free and searching books for answers, but He loved me through it all and loves me today. Although I know people can and do change, there have been so many others whose hearts God had to change rather than whom they loved. It is just now I have learned to love myself and accept who I am.

Love is never wrong. Wasn't it Jesus Himself who said that those who are without sin should cast the first stone? Stones fell and were not thrown on that day. As the song goes, God accepts us *just as we are*. People also use the Old Testament to point out the abomination of homosexuality. Sodom and Gomorrah were destroyed not because of homosexuals but for immorality and because people were having orgies and asking to send out the angel who had been sent to the city so they could rape them. Also, if they want to use the Old Testament, then they need to utilize it all. Stoning children for disobeying, sacrificial lambs, what we eat, and so many more examples—those things passed away on the Cross. We were created in His image, and that is not just the image of a white heterosexual male.

My life has been full of monsters, some large and some small, but I had been able to overcome them in some way. Troubles abounded and tried to pull me down into the mire of hate, but I rose above it. Life handed me lemons, and I made lemonade. You can never go back and change your past, but you can learn to accept it and live with it. Forgiveness is more for yourself than for those you are forgiving. It doesn't mean forgetting because you will likely never forget what was done to you, but you can let go of the anger and bitterness in your heart so that you don't remain ensnared by those who hurt you. Don't give them any more power than they already had over you and your life! Do not make the same mistakes that were made with you. Be your own best friend. You may not always end up with a fairy-tale ending where you live happily ever after, but dragons can be slain, wars can be won, and those who live in dark castles can be rescued. Sometimes, dreams do ultimately come true. I was able to mount up on wings like an eagle, and I learned to fly!

About the Author

Robert Gatz has had essays published in a college textbook as well as several poems find their way into the written world. He lives happily, sharing his life with his three children and seven grandchildren as well as his partner of over twenty-five years. This book has been written to touch lives and lead people out of the darkness of abuse into the light of hope.

Printed in the USA
CPSIA information can be obtained
at www.ICGtesting.com
LVHW090237091024
793326LV00002B/283

9 798893 086126